PARVITAS MATERIAE IN SEXTO IN CONTEMPORARY CATHOLIC THOUGHT

Patrick J. Boyle, S.J.

UNIVERSITY
PRESS OF
AMERICA

LANHAM • NEW YORK • LONDON

Copyright © 1987 by

University Press of America,® Inc.

4720 Boston Way
Lanham, MD 20706

3 Henrietta Street
London WC2E 8LU England

All rights reserved

Printed in the United States of America

British Cataloging in Publication Information Available

Library of Congress Cataloging in Publication Data

Boyle, Patrick J., 1932-
 Parvitas materiae in sexto in contemporary Catholic thought.

 Bibliography: p.
 Includes index.
 1. Sex—Religious aspects—Catholic Church—History of doctrines—20th century.   2. Christian ethics—Catholic authors.   3. Catholic Church—Doctrines—History—20th century.   I. Title.
BX1795.S48B69   1987   241'.66   86-28095
ISBN 0-8191-5790-2 (alk. paper)
ISBN 0-8191-5791-0 (pbk. : alk. paper)

All University Press of America books are produced on acid-free paper which exceeds the minimum standards set by the National Historical Publication and Records Commission.

This book is dedicated to

Reverend Peter D. Fox, S.J.

A priest of great spirit and even greater courage.

TABLE OF CONTENTS

Introduction		1
Chapter 1	Historical Overview of the Traditional Teaching	9
Chapter II	The Teaching of the Approved Authors Prior to Vatican II	31
Chapter III	A Re-Evaluation of Moral Theology in the Theological Climate Subsequent to Vatican II	45
Capter IV	Methodological Objections to the Traditional Teaching of No Parvity of Matter	67
Chapter V	A Critical Evaluation of the Traditional and Contemporary Teachings on Parvity of Matter in Sexual Sins	95
Bibliography		114
Index		121

Preface

There can be no doubt that the Second Vatican Council was the single most important event for the Roman Catholic Church in the twentieth century. The <u>aggiornamento</u>, mandated by the Council, was needed to update a church which had become steeped in late medieval traditions and practices.

Roman Catholic theology was also a victim of this malaise. Because of an anti-modernist mentality, which prevailed during the first half of the twentieth century, and because of a non-collegial understanding of authority, the academic freedom, necessary in any pursuit of truth, was for the most part stifled. Catholic teaching was to be merely passed on from generation to generation. It was never to be questioned. Vatican II changed this mind-set. It opened the door. It gave theologians the academic freedom to question, to speak out, to experiment. Theologians were able to look at traditional Catholic thought, past and present, with a critical eye without being branded disloyal.

Spurred by the enthusiasm of the Second Vatican Council, I have chosen in this book to examine one of those time-bound teachings in the Catholic tradition -- no parvity of matter in sins against the sixth and ninth commandments. The question is not a burning issue in Catholic theology. Indeed, I am fully convinced that most Catholic lay people are not in the least familiar with the question. Nevertheless, it is still considered Roman Catholic theological teaching as witnessed in the 1975 document, <u>Persona Humana</u>. In the spirit of Vatican II, the no parvity of <u>matter in re sexuali</u> should be reassessed. If, for no other reason, it should be examined to see whether or not it is worthy to be called Catholic teaching. If not, it should be purged.

Even though the title page of this work lists only one author, there are many other individuals who deserve equal billing. Without the support, encouragement, and expertise of these following people, this book would never have been.

I am most grateful to Father Edmund Fortman, S.J. for his encouragement and his advice. His knowledge of theology and his lucid explanations made this work seem very easy. I am grateful to Father Walter Krolikowski, S.J. of Loyola University. His critical reading of the original manuscript and his excellent suggestions were most helpful. Above all, I am most grateful to Dr. Dennis Doherty of Marquette University who was the guiding light of the whole project. His cajoling, encouragement, and theological insights enabled me to clarify my own thoughts, and to "write" for publication. He is a good friend.

Finally, I am most grateful to the real workers. I am most grateful to Mrs. Eileen Juchcinski for her support and encouragement, to Mrs. Donna Juchcinski, Mrs. Barbara Spyra, and Mrs. Leanne Meyer for their typing and retyping the manuscript many, many times. I am most grateful to Mrs. Evelyn Congiusti and Mrs. Lauren Zubert for editing the manuscript and preparing it for publication. The patience and charity of all these real "workers" border on the heroic.

                                      Patrick J. Boyle, S.J.
                                      University of St. Mary of the Lake
                                      Mundelein, Illinois

Introduction

In pre-Vatican II moral manuals of Catholic theology sexuality was viewed as essentially procreative. All sexual behavior was judged good or bad in relationship to this procreative dimension. The unitive aspect of sexuality was all but ignored. Vatican II was the turning point in Catholic moral thought on sexuality when it abandoned the traditional ranking of the ends of marriage. As a result, sexual morality was no longer centered solely on the procreative aspect. The aspect of the love which exists between spouses received equal emphasis. In the documents, Gaudium et Spes and Humanae Vitae, the papal magisterium insists on the fruitful aspect of human love, but not to the exclusion of the interpersonal dimension of human sexuality.

This change of direction on the part of the papal magisterium requires Catholic moralists to re-evaluate many of the traditional moral teachings on sexuality, which was based solely on the procreative dimension of sexuality. One such teaching which has to be reconsidered is the gravity of matter in sexual sins. Prior to Vatican II it had been common teaching among theologians that the moral object in sexual sins admitted of no parvity.

Apart from the ethical reasons for treating this topic, for example: lack of a theological basis in Scripture which could give some credibility to the teaching, a new understanding of the natural law and its resulting new methodology, and the prohibition by external authority of the free theological development of the teaching, the pastoral effects of the teaching are far reaching, especially for the correct understanding of human sexuality. This fact by itself makes the topic worthy of treatment. Since sexuality is a good and the ordinary means through which a husband and wife express their love for one another, it is most important that all aspects of sexuality be presented in their truest light. To brand the matter of sexual sins as serious leads to the fostering of a wrong attitude towards sex in the minds of the married and the unmarried. One can easily imply that the very acts which are necessary to maintain and to strengthen union and love within marriage are sordid and dirty. An attitude of fear and suspicion towards sex can develop.

The traditional teaching of no parvity of matter in sexual sins enhances an already exaggerated emphasis on sexual activity in the minds of the faithful. Because of this undue emphasis, the faithful have become pre-occupied over the years with the notion of avoiding sins of a sexual nature as opposed to those sins which admit of parvity of matter.

In most moral manuals prior to Vatican II sin is generally defined as the free transgression of the divine law. Three elements are listed for every sin: the transgression of a law whether actual or putative, knowledge of the transgression even if only confused, and free consent to the act.[1]

Every sin can be considered from two different aspects: objectively, the act itself; or subjectively, the act as it appears imputable in the consciousness of the individual who performs the act. The performance of an objectively evil act apart from the imputable elements is called "material" sin. Sin is considered "formal" when the conditions necessary for subjective imputability, namely knowledge of the transgression and free consent, are present. The manualists taught that the determination of the objective sinfulness of an action is made on the basis of divine revelation as interpreted by the magisterium of the Church and on the basis of the rational analysis of the nature of the act. The determination of subjective imputability is a psychological question. In contemporary moral theology with its existential emphasis, interest tends to center on the subjective.[2]

Pre-Vatican II moralists taught that material sin draws its malice from any one of three possible sources: the matter; an added circumstance which in some way further specifies the act; or the intention of the one who performs the act. Since the topic treated in this work deals with parvity of matter in sexual sins, the first font of morality in material sin, the matter, will be the main consideration.

There is no question that the manualists considered the matter of sin as a font of morality separate from the fonts of circumstance and intention. Considered abstractly, the matter consists of the act itself such as to eat, to sleep, to read. More specifically, however, in moral manuals and in magisterial literature matter included both the act and the object of the act. Thus, the matter in the act of stealing is the taking of another person's money.[3] The manualists further taught that the matter of sin can admit of moral evil in itself apart from a consideration of circumstance and intention. This evil matter can be quantified as either serious or light.[4]

The manualists classified sin according to the seriousness of the matter. Mortal sins <u>ex toto genere suo</u> are sins whose matter is so evil that there is no possible situation in which gravity of the evil can be lessened. The matter is intrinsically evil. Mortal sins <u>ex genere suo</u> are sins whose matter can be either serious or light depending upon the circumstances which specify the act. In this category sins within the same species may be mortal or venial depending upon the seriousness of the matter. For example, the degree of malice of the sin of theft depends not only on whether something valuable or something petty is taken, but more precisely on the person from whom the object is stolen. If a petty amount is taken from a rich person, then the matter is considered light. On the other hand, the same amount if taken from a pauper is considered serious matter. Venial sins <u>ex</u> <u>toto</u> <u>genere</u> <u>suo</u> are sins whose matter is always light as long as there are no added circumstances that might change the species of the act.[5]

It has been a long established teaching in pre-Vatican II moral theology that the matter in every sexual sin falls into the <u>ex</u> <u>toto</u> <u>genere</u> <u>suo</u> category. For centuries moral theologians and the papal magisterium of the Church held that there can be no parvity of matter in sins against the sixth and ninth commandments.

In 1935, Henry Davis, S.J. wrote that this established teaching of the magisterium was a closed issue. The teaching was universally held by all reputable moral theologians. In his opinion the discussion was closed because of this unanimous agreement among theologians and because of the intrinsic reasons for the teaching. He states that the evidence in support of the teaching was so compelling that no theologian would venture to deny it. Nevertheless, Davis writes that the teaching was not always universally accepted. In the past there were some who held the contrary position: Fumo (1545), Martinus Magister (1482), Ledesma (1616), Araujo (1664), Marchant (1661). However, even in their time, according to Davis, theologians who taught parvity of matter in sexual sins were in minority. The greater number of theologians held and taught the doctrine of no parvity of matter.[6]

John R. Connery, S.J. supports the findings of Davis. He writes that the teaching of parvity of matter in sexual sins had some proponents in the fifteenth and sixteenth centuries. However, in 1612 after the famous decree of the Jesuit General, Claude Acquaviva, he states that this view met with increasing opposition until by the middle of the seventeenth century it no longer had any supporters. Connery, in 1948, agreed with Davis that it would be rash to teach or even hold parvity of matter in sexual sins.[7]

Throughout the centuries of development of the traditional teaching on parvity of matter, the magisterium never directly addressed the question. There was no official conclusive statement, affirming or denying the teaching of no parvity of matter in every type of sexual sin. Until recent years the silence of the magisterium was accepted by theologians as affirming the traditional teaching. In 1975, the papal magisterium spoke in support of the teaching. The validity of the no parvity of matter teaching was officially endorsed by the Sacred Congregation for the Doctrine of the Faith. In the document, Persona Humana, the Congregation states that according to Christian Tradition, right reason, and the Church's teaching every direct violation of the moral order of sexuality is objectively serious because in the moral order of sexuality such high values of human life are involved.[8] It is true that Persona Humana cites earlier statements and decrees of the magisterium in support of this teaching of no parvity of matter in sexual sins. These references, however, do not actually treat of the subject. They rather emphasize the sacredness and right use of sex in and out of marriage. One might infer from these references that the magisterium meant to imply the no parvity of matter teaching. Nevertheless, it does not necessarily follow from the wording.

In spite of this recent pronouncement of the magisterium of the Church, that unanimity of thought, which was so evident in the past, in reference to the traditional teaching on parvity of matter is no longer present in contemporary moral theology. This is due to the modern-day movement away from a natural law/act-oriented moral theology to a natural law/person-centered moral theology. The traditional position of the magisterium on the seriousness of matter in sins against the sixth and ninth commandments is being seriously questioned in many contemporary Catholic theological writings. Charles E. Curran is one such theologian who questions the traditional teaching. He writes that the development of this teaching was due to purely extrinsic reasons. Church authorities prevented any free discussion of the topic for centuries. Consequently, the teaching was never open to proper theological method and development. Proper method in theology requires that both sides of a theological question be considered. Dialectic is a necessary tool in order to arrive at a proper understanding of a theological teaching. It is obvious that without a position counter-position approach the development of any theological truth is totally one-sided and its objective validity is certainly questionable. It is precisely because of this lack of proper theological method that Curran believes many contemporary moral theologians rightly reject the traditional teaching of no parvity of matter in sexual sins.[9]

It is not the purpose of this work to trace the historical development of the traditional teaching on parvity of matter in sexual sins from its formulation to its general acceptance by moral theologians. Such an approach has been ably treated by such theologians as Karl-Heinz Kleber and John R. Connery.[10] These men traced the historical development of the traditional teaching from the time of St. Thomas Aquinas till the middle of the eighteenth century when it had become firmly entrenched in theology as solid doctrine.

The main issue under consideration in this work is a critical analysis of the recent approach to parvity of matter (that in the area of sexuality there is a smallness of matter) in the writings of certain contemporary moral theologians. As stated above, among these contemporary moral theologians a change from traditional teaching has been noted. Some theologians are still holding to the traditional teaching, others are arguing the possibility of parvity of matter in sexual sins. Since any change of a traditional teaching in theology is worthy of investigation, in this work we will focus primarily on that change from no parvity to parvity of matter in sexual sins and will investigate the events and the new theological insights which laid the foundation for the change. It will also consider the theological arguments which both the manualists and the contemporary theologians set forth in support of their respective teachings on the matter. In our investigation when the word contemporary is used, it is to be understood as that time from the end of Vatican II till the present day.

Nevertheless, in order to arrive at a proper perspective of the traditional teaching as well as a contemporary position on parvity of matter in sexual sins, our focus will also center on the writings of some prominent moral theologians prior to Vatican II. This procedure will point up that tradition from which the contemporary position developed and give the reader a more comprehensive view of the parvity of matter question.

With this procedure in mind our investigation begins, as its point of departure, with the writings of St. Thomas Aquinas and carries through to the present day. Since the dissertation is not an historical presentation, obviously not all the moral theologians who have ever written on the subject of parvity of matter in the pre- and post-Vatican II era will be considered. The vast number of such prohibits any exhaustive presentation. Besides, such a listing of these theologians is not necessary to accomplish the purpose of our undertaking. To arrive at a clear and proper understanding of the change from the traditional teaching to the contemporary approach to parvity of matter in sexual sins, only the thoughts and arguments of a few prominent theologians on both sides of the question will be required.

The material in this treatise is divided into five chapters. The first chapter considers an historical overview of the traditional teaching on parvity of matter. The arguments and thoughts of a few representative moral theologians who contributed to the development of this traditional doctrine will be presented. The arguments which those theologians used in support of their respective positions will be considered. The reader will be given the opportunity to see the parvity of matter question in its initial stages and the process of development towards the denial of parvity of matter in sexual sins. The second chapter will present the position of five pre-Vatican II prominent moral theologians who advocate the traditional teaching of no parvity of matter. Their arguments in favor of this traditional teaching will be considered. A firmly entrenched teaching of the traditional position and the theological arguments upon which it rests will come to light. Chapter Three will look at the events and new theological insights which set the stage for the development of the new approach to the question of parvity of matter in sexual sins. This chapter will also answer the question of "how" the change came about. In this chapter a clearer perspective of the contemporary approach will surface, thereby giving the reader a better overall understanding of the approach. Chapter Four will present the thoughts on parvity of matter in sexual sins as found in the writings of five contemporary moral theologians who are more or less representative of theologians espousing the new approach. The arguments of these five theologians in support of their position will also be considered. In Chapter Five the weaknesses of both the traditional teaching and the contemporary approach on parvity of matter in sexual sins will be presented and critiqued by moral theologians on both sides of the question. Finally, in this chapter the author of this treatise will give an evaluation of the two approaches and their pastoral consequences, as well as his thoughts on whether or not there can be parvity of matter in sexual sins.

Since the term, venereal pleasure, plays such an important part in the writings of pre-Vatican II moral theologians, it might be well at the outset to define the term and also define the two other pleasures identified in the sensitive appetite of man. This is necessary because in our investigation we will find that at times those who admit parvity of matter in the area of sexuality are really referring to sensual pleasure.

In the sensitive appetite of man three types of pleasures can be identified. The pleasure that is experienced when either the internal or external senses of a person are joined to their proper objects is called sensitive. Such pleasure that results from warmth, coolness, pleasant taste or odor, soothing music is listed as sensitive pleasure. Sensual pleasure is that which arises in the various senses of an individual from objects which of themselves are apt to cause venereal pleasure. A lover's kiss or embrace, a lover's physical presence, light caressing are considered as causing sensual pleasure. Venereal pleasure is that pleasure that is proper to the generative act either in its beginning stages or in its completion.[11]

It should also be pointed out that the discussion at times shifts from a consideration of parvity of matter in venereal pleasure to a consideration of parvity of matter in sexual sins. Even though this occurs, the substance of the question remains the same because, according to the manualists in whose works this interchange often takes place, the act and the pleasure are one and the same, but under different aspects. Pleasure is good or bad depending on whether the act from which it derives is good or bad. Consequently, to speak of parvity of matter in venereal pleasure or parvity of matter in sexual sins is basically the same question.

Since the magisterium of the Church plays such an important part in this matter and since a new understanding of the magisterium has developed in modern day theology, it will be well at the outset to define the term as understood in this work. In this treatise, the term magisterium is to be understood in the neo-Scholastic sense. Around the second half of the nineteenth century theologians of the Roman School taught that the pope and the bishops possessed a unique privilege. As successors of the Apostles, they were endowed with the "charism of truth." They were entrusted with transmitting the truth of revelation to future generations. All others who participated in this function, especially theologians, were not members of the magisterium. They played only a subordinate and instrumental role. Thus, according to the neo-Scholastics, the true teachers were the bishops whose competency to teach was not the result of study and learning, but merely from their elevation to the episcopacy.

As a result of this understanding of the magisterium, pre-Vatican II teachings were heavily juridicized. The response to a magisterial teaching was not understanding, but rather obedience. The norm for an authentic teaching was whether or not it emanated from those holding jurisdiction. Accordingly, in many of the textbooks of this era magisterial teaching was nothing more than an act of jurisdiction. Thus, instead of enlightening the mind as teaching is supposed to do, an obligation of obedience was imposed on the will.[12]

1 Heribert Jone, O.F.M. Cap., Moral Theology, Trans. Urban
  Adelman, O.F.M. Cap. (Westminster, Maryland: The Newman
  Press, 1960), p. 46.

2 I. McGinnis, "Sin", in the New Catholic Encyclopedia,
  Vol. 13, (New York: McGraw-Hill Book Company, 1967), p. 241.

3 Eduardus Genicot, S.J., Theologiae Moralis Institutiones,
  6th edition, Vol. 1, (Bruxellis: A. Dewit, 1909), p. 34.

4 Daniel Maguire takes exception to this understanding of
  moral matter. He writes that no fixed moral value of
  matter can be assessed until all circumstances surrounding
  the act have been examined and judged in relationship
  to one another. In his opinion the concept of moral matter
  apart from a consideration of circumstance and motive
  stems from a misunderstanding of St. Thomas Aquinas' treatment
  of the topic in his Summa, I-II, 18, a.2. cf. Daniel Maguire,
  The Moral Choice (New York: Doubleday and Co., Inc., 1978),
  p. 183 n. 16.

5 Jone, op. cit., pp. 46-47.

6 Henry Davis, S.J., Moral and Pastoral Theology, Vol. II,
  (New York: Sheed and Ward, 1935), pp. 180-181.

7 John R. Connery, S.J., The Morality of Incomplete Venereal
  Pleasure, an unpublished doctoral dissertation, (Rome,
  1948), pp. 276-278.

8 Sacred Congregation for the Doctrine of the Faith, "Declaration
  on Certain Questions Concerning Sexual Ethics", Catholic
  Mind 74 (April, 1976): 59.

9 Charles E. Curran, Issues in Sexual and Medical Ethics
  (Notre Dame, Ind.: University of Notre Dame Press, 1978),
  pp. 45-46.

10 Karl-Heinz Kleber, De Parvitate Materiae in Sexto
   (Regensburg: Verlag Friedrich Pustet, 1971) and
   John R. Connery, S.J., op. cit.

11 H. Noldin, S.J. and A. Schmitt, S.J., Summa Theologiae
   Moralis: De Principiis (Innsbruck: F. Rauch, 1940) pp. 9-10.

12 Avery Dulles, "The Theologians and the Magisterium," in
   Proceedings of the Catholic Theological Society of America
   31 (June, 1976): 238-239. Cf. also John P. Boyle, "The
   Ordinary Magisterium: Towards a History of the Concept"
   Heythrop Journal Vol. 20 (October, 1979) pp. 380-398 and
   Vol. 21 (January, 1980) pp. 14-29.

**Bellarmine Jesuit Retreat House
Men's Retreat
January 18-20, 2013**

Letting God Find You in All Things

**Conference # 6
The Paschal Mystery**

"The Lord gave, and the Lord has taken away; blessed be the name of the Lord."
- Job 1:21

"In the Cross God takes on the pain of humanity and of our history. The paradox is that through involvement with the most negative side of human history, a death in failure, God opens up for history a new hope."
- Philip Sheldrake, SJ

"It belongs to the Passion to ask for grief with Christ in grief, anguish with Christ in anguish, tears and interior pain at such great pain which Christ suffered for me."
- Sp.Ex. # 203

The Cross is understood only in light of the Incarnation.

The spirituality of the Passion cannot be reduced to pious meditation but must consist in following the path of Christ in our concrete situation.

True joy—anchored in God's character—cannot be separated from sorrow.

"In the light of this truth, all those who suffer can feel called to share in the work of redemption accomplished by means of the cross. To share in the cross of Christ means to believe in the saving power of the sacrifice which every believer can offer together with the Redeemer. Suffering then casts off the mantle of absurdity which seems to cover it. It acquires a profound dimension and reveals its creative meaning and value. It could then be said that it changes the scenario of existence, from which the destructive power of evil is ever farther removed, precisely because suffering bears its copious fruits...Could not one find here the answer which humanity awaits today? It can be received only from Christ crucified, the holy one who suffers. He can penetrate the heart of the most painful human problems, because he already stands beside all who suffer and who ask him for an awakening of new hope."

-Pope John Paul II, General Audience, November 9, 1988

Suggestions for prayer: one of the Passion narratives

- Matthew 27: 32-50
- Mark 15: 21-37
- Luke 23: 26-49
- John 19: 16-30

Pray for the grace to remain with Christ in his Passion.

Notes:

Chapter I

Historical Overview of the Traditional Teaching

The manualists' teaching of no parvity of matter in the sixth and ninth commandments is the product of many centuries of historical development. One way to gain the proper understanding of this teaching is to view its development at various stages in the writings of prominent theologians of the past few centuries. Karl-Heinz Kleber rightly points out in his work, <u>De Parvitate Materiae in Sexto</u>, that the denial of parvity of matter in the sixth and ninth commandments was held in practice many years before the actual principles were formulated.[1]

Any treatment of the subject of parvity of matter can conveniently begin with St. Thomas Aquinas. Even though he did not treat of the matter specifically in reference to the sixth and ninth commandments, still he formulated the distinctions and the general principles upon which subsequent moral theologians built their theories.

From his <u>Commentary on the Second Book of the Sentences</u> one can conclude that St. Thomas does not allow for parvity of matter in any sin which is of its very nature mortal. Sins of this type can be venial only because of some other reason. St. Thomas explains this by saying that the doer of the act is not capable of serious sin. The act is still in the incomplete stage and has not as yet reached the deliberate reason stage. According to St. Thomas only when a sinful act falls within the scope of deliberate reason is the possibility of serious sin possible. Before it reaches this stage, the sinful act is venial. Thus St. Thomas at this time of his theological thinking did not allow parvity of matter for any sin of its very nature mortal which had reached the stage of full deliberation.[2]

By 1265, St. Thomas broadened his notion of the incompleteness of an act to include the gravity of matter. In the <u>Summa</u> when discussing the question of avarice he writes that even though avarice is mortally sinful of its very nature, still it can be a venial sin because of the incompleteness of the act. In explaining this St. Thomas refers his readers to his treatise in the <u>Summa</u> on stealing.[3] In that treatise he makes the statement that reason does not consider the stealing of a small sum as important. Thus stealing a slight sum in St. Thomas's mind is excused from mortal sin not only because the act lacks full deliberation, but more precisely because of the light matter.[4]

St. Thomas further clarifies his thoughts in this area in his <u>De Malo</u> where he discusses the sins which spring from the capital vices. He says that one can commit venial sin even though these sins are considered mortal of its very nature because of the incompleteness of the act, which incompleteness can be due to one of two sources. The one source we discussed above. An act can be incomplete because it lacks full-deliberateness. In other words, it does not issue forth from deliberate reason. Thus, according to St. Thomas' theory, a sudden impulse to commit homicide or adultery is not a serious sin because the act is in its semi-deliberate stage. The second source that can influence the incompleteness of an act is the object itself, that is the lightness or seriousness of the matter. St. Thomas justifies this position by stating the same reason that he gave in the <u>Summa</u> -- reason considers that which is small as nothing.[5]

In <u>De Malo</u> St. Thomas applies this second understanding of the incompleteness of an act to the sins of envy,[6] anger,[7] and avarice.[8] He does not, however, extend this understanding to include sins of lust. When he treats the question of lust, he makes no mention of parvity of matter. All acts of lust involve serious matter.[9] Thus it would seem that St. Thomas, since he does not apply this second understanding of the incompleteness of an act when discussing sins of lust, does not hold parvity of matter in sins against the sixth and ninth commandments. The same holds true for libidinous kisses and embraces. St. Thomas makes no allowance for slight pleasure which would excuse from mortal sin.[10] In the <u>Summa</u> St. Thomas talks about the pleasure which arises from the <u>act</u> of fornication. He says that this pleasure can be a venial sin, not, however, by reason of parvity of matter. In this case he is referring to the act in its incomplete stage -- its semi-deliberate stage -- and not to lightness of the matter.[11]

For St. Thomas, therefore, all acts of lust are mortal sins of their very nature. The pleasure arising either from the acts themselves or the thoughts of them is seriously sinful. He makes no provision for light pleasure. Kisses and touches are in themselves indifferent acts. They become serious matter when directed towards the pleasure of fornication no matter how slight the pleasure. According to St. Thomas, therefore, the measure for determining the gravity of any particular sinful act is not the intensity of the pleasure enjoyed, but its relationship to a mortally sinful act. Once that relationship is established, the intensity of pleasure is not considered.

Even though St. Thomas was not specific in denying parvity of matter in the sixth and ninth commandments, Martinus Magister (1432-1482) was one of the first theologians to take issue with what he did say on the matter. He takes exception to St. Thomas's absolute statement that kisses and touches are mortal sins in so far as they are libidinous or in so far as they spring from some libidinous motive. Martinus disagrees with this statement because in his mind acts can be libidinous in two ways. In the first sense acts can be libidinous if indulged in for the purpose of inducing another to consent to some venereal or libidinous acts. Acts can be libidinous according to Martinus in a second way, namely if they are engaged in for the sake of the pleasure experienced in them. Martinus cites the kissing of one's sister as an example of this second type of libidinous act. Such a kiss is a pleasurable act but at the same time it is accompanied with a firm determination not to seduce her and never allow her to be seduced.[12]

Martinus states that this latter type of libidinous act can certainly be dangerous. It can be the occasion of sin or an incentive toward it. One is always confronted with the danger of weakening. Hence, these types of libidinous acts are as steps on the road to sin. However, in spite of all these dangers, he says that these libidinous acts indulged in for the pleasure alone cannot be called mortal sins. He bases his claim for this statement on the fact that neither the pleasure nor the acts are forbidden. When St. Paul writes about the malice of these acts, Martinus says that he calls them evil because they are already referred to the act of fornication. However, the libidinous act in his second sense is not the same. There is no question of referral. One does not go beyond the pleasure of touch itself. Martinus says, therefore, that these acts are not serious sins because of the possibility of further sin. If such a danger should constitute serious sin, then all communication with women would be forbidden and mortally sinful.[13]

Martinus refuses to accept the Scripture text, Matthew 5:28, as an argument against his position. The text reads that anyone who thinks lustfully about a woman has already sinned in his heart. Martinus distinguishes between looks which are antecedent to the consent and in no way directed toward it and those which involve consent to the act. The Matthean text refers to those acts which involve this consent. These acts are serious sins.[14]

Nor can one, according to Martinus, use St. Thomas's statement in his <u>De Malo</u> concerning the gravity of all kisses, touches and embraces as an argument against his position. He simply refuses to accept it. Martinus denies the universality of the statement that all sins of lust are mortal sins. He supports this with an example taken from the married state. He does admit, however, that both consent to the pleasure and consent to the act of mortal sin are mortally sinful.[15]

Martinus's position is extremely liberal. One could understand and allow his teaching if he limited it to the pleasure which is derived from kissing one's sister. Such an act, though pleasurable, is not a mortal sin. However, to say that the pleasure which arises from kissing and embracing becomes serious matter only when the ultimate goal is the act of fornication or some other species of lust and when this is the explicit intention of the agent is to go beyond all previous teaching.

It is generally agreed that the first theologian to affirm the existence of parvity of matter in the sixth and ninth commandments was Martin of Azpilcueta, the famous Doctor Navarrus (1495-1586).16 This distinction could have gone to Martinus Magister but, as Charles Curran writes, there is some problem with what Martinus meant by the term, libidinous.17 There is no such ambiguity in the writings of Doctor Navarrus. His teaching in this area developed to such a degree that in the end he made this positive, though qualified, statement about parvity of matter -- <u>videtur posse dari</u>. In his mind there can be no parvity of matter in reference to the act of intercourse. The pleasure arising from this act will always be serious matter. But the Doctor Navarrus does not see why one could not admit the possibility of parvity of matter in the venereal pleasure which arises from sexual thoughts or touches. He centers his argument around the analogy with the other commandments. Since the other commandments admit of parvity of matter, why should the sixth and ninth commandments be different? 18

One of the leading theologians of the sixteenth century was a staunch defender of parvity of matter in the sixth and ninth commandments. Thomas Sanchez, S.J. (1550-1610), was among the last of the Jesuit moralists who could speak his mind freely on the subject. Sanchez defined venereal pleasure as that carnal pleasure which is experienced in the genital area of the body when sexually aroused. He identifies two types of venereal pleasure. The one type is that which arises from the act of intercourse and is deliberately sought. The second type arises from acts without any intention on the part of the agent either for intercourse or its pleasure. Sanchez distinguished venereal pleasure from sensible pleasure which is derived from touches and looks due to a certain proportion between an object and the sense organ contracted.19

With these definitions of terms in mind Sanchez then presents his thoughts on parvity of matter. All sensible pleasure that arises from kisses and touches independent of any subjective thought of fornication or its pleasure is mortally sinful. In holding this Sanchez is going against the teaching of many theologians of his and past time, who consider such acts to be indifferent in themselves. He holds this rigorous doctrine because he believes that acts of kissing and embracing when indulged in for pleasure are intrinsically ordered to intercourse. In his opinion these acts are the beginnings of intercourse because by nature they cause notable excitement in the genital region of the body.[20]

Even though he takes a rather rigorous position concerning the gravity of matter of kisses and embraces, Sanchez does not deny the possibility of parvity of matter in reference to such acts. There can be, he writes, light matter in these acts as long as there is no danger of orgasm or no danger of consent to a further more serious carnal act. Sanchez states that there can be no parvity of matter in regards to the complete act, for example, the act of fornication. On the other hand, there can be light matter in dealing with the pleasures which arise from incomplete acts such as from acts of touch and thought. Like Doctor Navarrus, Sanchez sees no reason why parvity of matter should be allowed in the other commandments but not allowed in sins against the sixth and ninth commandments. Thus Sanchez differs from many of his contemporaries who admit the seriousness of kisses and touches not by reason of the gravity of matter, but rather because of the proximate danger of orgasm or consent on the part of the subject. He believes that the matter itself is serious or light independent of the danger of orgasm and consent. He does not rule out parvity of matter. In his mind, if a venial sin is committed by kissing and embracing, the reason is because the matter is light and not necessarily because the danger of consent and orgasm is removed.[21]

There seems to be some confusion in Sanchez's mind as to the extent of parvity of matter. In one instance, he says that kisses and embraces are mortally sinful when indulged in for the sake of sensible pleasure and at the same time that slight venereal pleasure is only venially sinful. These two statements can be reconciled if one realizes that he is not distinguishing between types of pleasure. With this supposition in mind Sanchez's teaching concerning the morality of kissing and embracing can be explained as follows. Such acts which are sought for pleasure are mortally sinful. In this case, he makes no distinction between sensible or strictly venereal pleasure. Later, as was pointed out above, he refined his teaching and allowed slight pleasure, again without distinguishing the types, to be considered a venial sin. Such acts, he writes, indulged in out of levity or jest, even with the intent of enjoying venereal pleasure, are light matter, provided the danger of orgasm and the danger of consent to further carnal acts be absent. Sanchez held parvity of matter in such acts because he feels that the pleasure experienced in these frivolous and jocular acts is so slight that it can in no way be considered serious matter.[22]

Thus for Sanchez it would seem that the gravity of the sin of touch depends upon the type of touch. Light touches indulged in jokingly or out of levity rather than out of a desire for venereal pleasure are not serious matter. Even if the pleasure is deliberately sought, these acts are light matter as long as the pleasure is slight. Prolonged kisses and embraces are serious matter, since the pleasure arising from them in his mind is the beginning of intercourse. One could really say that Sanchez admits parvity of matter not in regard to the degree of venereal pleasure but rather in regard to the seriousness of the act.

In treating of the morality of looks Sanchez writes more about parvity of matter. He says that the venereal pleasure that arises from looks is only slight matter since it is not ordered to venereal acts as are touches.[23] The gravity of light touches and looks is similar. The pleasure arising from both is so slight that it can be considered light matter. Thus Sanchez writes that to look at the arms, legs, or other parts of another person's body is not serious matter even though there is some venereal pleasure involved unless the danger of going further is present. In Sanchez's mind the pleasure is slight and not ordered to other venereal acts.[24]

Some time between the publication of his De Matrimonio and that of his Opus Morale Sanchez is said to have rethought his teaching on parvity of matter.[25] He writes that Clement VIII and Paul V approved the teaching that there is no parvity of matter in regard to libidinous kisses and embraces. Sanchez was in complete agreement. He retracts his position on parvity of matter, because this allows his teaching to be more in conformity with the teaching of the Holy See. He writes also that his retraction is more in conformity to the truth, namely any venereal pleasure deliberately accepted, notwithstanding the danger of orgasm or further consent, is mortally sinful.[26]

There is some doubt in regard to the authenticity of Sanchez's retraction. His Opus Morale was published posthumously and the retraction in De Matrimonio appeared only in editions published after his death.[27]

The turning point in reference to parvity of matter in the sixth and ninth commandments occurred in 1612 with the proclamation of the decree of Claude Acquaviva, the General of the Society of Jesus. Up to that time the Holy See had not as yet addressed the question of parvity of matter in sexual sins directly. After 1612, with few exceptions it was more or less a closed question. In 1612, Acquaviva issued a decree aimed at those who taught that some slight pleasure in re venerea deliberately sought could be excused from mortal sin. His decree forbade all the members of the Society of Jesus from teaching this doctrine in any form. It further forbade Jesuits from showing themselves in any way supportive towards it or from counseling according to it.28 Acquaviva issued the decree for two reasons. The first was that the opinion in favor of parvity of matter in his mind was harmful to the reputation of the Society. He also believed that the purity of life which the Society demanded of its members and its externs required such a teaching. His second reason for promulgating the decree was that the learned and authoritative fathers of the Society with whom he had consulted in this matter considered it in practice to be a teaching totally false and very much opposed to the virtue of chastity. These authoritative and learned fathers arrived at this conclusion because of the inherent danger in holding the contrary doctrine and because of the impossibility of distinguishing in practice between light and grave matter.29

Acquaviva was so insistent on the prohibition that he attached severe censures to the violation on the decree. The decree bound all members of the Society under the vow of holy obedience and its violation was subject to a number of penalties including excommunication.30 It also imposed upon all Jesuits by virtue of holy obedience the obligation of revealing the names of those Jesuits who failed to observe the decree.31

In the decree and accompanying letter to the whole Society, Acquaviva noted that he had hoped for a future more authoritative statement on the matter from the Holy See. He wrote in the accompanying letter that he knew how offensive the teaching of parvity of matter was to Paul V and that the doctrine he put forth in the decree was actually the teaching of the Holy See.32

Actually, the decree did not prevent further discussion of the matter. Since the wording of the decree was in general terms, a certain amount of confusion resulted. The decree failed to define a libidinous touch and did not distinguish between touches and looks. It talked in generic terms, res venerea. The acts from which the pleasure arises received little mention. Even though the term venereal pleasure was not mentioned by name, it is generally taken as such by most Jesuit moralists. Other types of pleasure are not according to them included under the ban.

The decree did not treat of the speculative order. It did not consider whether or not venereal pleasure in theory could admit of parvity of matter. However, one can infer from the all-embracing tone of the decree that it forbade the teaching even in the speculative order. It forbade the teaching, ulla ratione.

Since Jesuit moralists dominated the field of moral theology at that time, the decree for all practical purposes ended all discussion of the matter. The contrary opinion would no longer be taught. There were a few Jesuits who taught the doctrine under a different guise. Adam Tanner, S.J., and Roderico de Arriaga, S.J., felt that they could legitimately distinguish between pleasure deliberately sought and pleasure merely accepted, since the decree only mentioned the former words. This approach was short-lived. The decree was at a later date extended to include the prohibition of pleasure merely accepted also.[33]

Even though Jesuit moralists were reduced to silence by Acquaviva's decree, other theologians took up the question. Juan Caramuel (de Lobkowitz), O.Cist., treats the matter in his work, <u>Commentarius in Regulam D. Benedicti</u>. In this work, published in 1640, he states that in matters of a venereal nature there is parvity of matter. He offers two reasons for his position. His first reason is the standard one. In all the other commandments there is parvity of matter, so why should not the same be true in the sixth and ninth commandments? Caramuel's second reason for his position on parvity of matter concerns the make-up of venereal matter. Matter which is by nature light cannot be morally grave. In his opinion there can be venereal pleasure that is by nature light. Therefore he concludes that there does exist venereal pleasure which admits of parvity of matter.[34] Caramuel develops his argument in his later work, <u>Theologia Moralis Fundamentalis</u>.

After affirming the existence of parvity of matter in the sixth and ninth commandments, Caramuel proceeds to give his theory concerning the distinction between light and serious matter. He says that some theologians base the distinction on the quality of the acts. For example, hand holding, foot play, and kissing are light matter as long as there is no serious sin. Caramuel had a different method of distinguishing light from serious matter. He employs a quantitative measure. Any pleasure which is less than one-eighth the amount necessary to produce an orgasm should be considered light matter. Any amount that is more is serious matter. In reality, however, Caramuel states that the question of measuring light and serious matter is meaningless since all acts in matters sexual are serious because the danger of consenting to serious sin is always present.[35]

In his later work, <u>Theologia Moralis Fundamentalis</u>, published in 1675, Caramuel still held the position of parvity of matter, but he refined his thoughts somewhat. He made a distinction between the speculative and practical orders. In the former he believed that Peter could touch the foot of a woman with his foot without exposing himself to further sin. To state it another way, Caramuel believed that Paul can cast a fleeting glance at a passing woman without the desire of proceeding any further. He concludes therefore that one could admit the possibility of light and serious matter in the speculative order.36 In the practical order, however, Caramuel states that there is no parvity of matter. In his mind the danger of proceeding further is always present.37 Thus for Caramuel if one looks only at the venereal pleasure, abstracting from the inherent danger connected with it, one can admit of parvity of matter. However, in the practical order because the pleasure and the danger of proceeding to further sin are so intimately connected there can be, in his opinion, no parvity of matter in the sixth and ninth commandments.38

Caramuel cites forty-nine authors who hold parvity of matter in venereal pleasure outside of marriage. Some, he says, hold it only in the speculative order, and not in the practical order.39

Juan de Cardenas, S.J. (1613-1684) was strongly critical of Caramuel's teaching and his accuracy. He writes that Caramuel cited authors who admitted venial sin in matters of lust in general without referring specifically to venereal pleasure. Cardenas says that of the forty-nine theologians cited by Caramuel as holding parvity of matter, forty of them in no way teach the doctrine. Of the nine remaining, only five teach it with certainty: James Marchantius, Martinus Magister, Thomas Sanchez, Lublin and F. Araujo.40

Cardenas's main concern in this matter was to reassert the authority of Jesuit moralists. Since the decree of Acquaviva, Caramuel stated that they were sorely lacking in discussing this matter of parvity of matter. He felt that obedience to the edict stifled any theological reasoning on their part. Cardenas disagreed strongly and rigorously in responding to Caramuel.

First of all, Cardenas claimed that the decree really reflected the teaching of the great Jesuit moralists of the time, since Acquaviva would not have acted without previously consulting them. Secondly, the content of the decree was broadened by Vincent Caraffa, S.J. and in 1649 was submitted to the Ninth General Congregation, which was composed of representation from the entire Society of Jesus. Obedience certainly came into play according to Cardenas, but he says that the moralists of the Society did not cease theologizing. They continued to develop new arguments in support of the teaching.41

Cardenas gives three arguments in favor of the teaching of no parvity of matter in venereal pleasure. He appeals in the first place to the argument used by Acquaviva in the decree. Cardenas stated that in the seeking of venereal pleasure one is not able to fix a definite point beyond which he will not proceed. The reason for this lies in the fact that as soon as one causes venereal pleasure, immediately a "co-cause" is present which is a vehement appetite for more of that pleasure. Cardenas states that it is not possible to act otherwise. The only way to impede augmentation of the pleasure is to abstain from seeking the pleasure no matter how slight.[42]

Cardenas's second argument in support of his position centered around the proximate-occasion-of-sin approach. Whenever one deliberately seeks venereal pleasure no matter how slight, he exposes himself to the danger of falling into serious sin.[43]

Cardenas's third argument is based on the rules governing a doubtful conscience. If one, he says, is stealing a petty amount of money and has a practical doubt about the lightness of the act he is performing, he sins seriously because he exposes himself to the possibility that the sum of money taken could be so great as to involve grave matter. According to Cardenas, all theologians hold this. Cardenas uses this same argument in support of the traditional teaching on parvity of matter. He says that if one sins seriously when he has a practical doubt concerning the gravity of an act he is performing, then all the more so does one sin who has a practical doubt in ascertaining the lightness or seriousness of an act he intends to perform. One must resolve the doubt before performing the act. Cardenas believes that this is the common teaching of theologians. The line between light and serious matter is so fine, he says, that one can pass from one to the other without scarcely knowing it. He compares this transition to a spark falling into dry stalks. He says that even though one might wish to light only one stalk, it would be most difficult to control the fire from spreading to the other stalks. Thus, Cardenas concludes, in the practical order these arguments prove the absence of parvity of matter in the sixth and ninth commandments. He goes on further to say that this is a "most certain" doctrine among theologians.[44]

Claudius Lacroix, S.J. (1652-1714) brought no new insights to the discussion on parvity of matter. He supports the doctrine as put forth in the decree of Acquaviva. According to Lacroix, all venereal pleasure is serious matter for the unmarried. Therefore there can be no venereal pleasure so slight that it cannot be considered serious matter. He offers proof for his position. First of all, he says, Clement VIII and Paul V denounced all those who teach that passionate embraces and kisses are not serious matter if the venereal pleasure is not ordered to the completed act. He states that in his opinion many theologians feel this view to be condemned by the teaching of the Popes. There are some theologians who do not go that far. Lacroix says that they believe the Popes only denounced the teaching as wrong, temerarious, scandalous. His second reason for supporting the thesis of no parvity of matter in sexual sins is the teleological aspect of the pleasure. He says all venereal pleasure is ordered to the completed act. Therefore, according to Lacroix, even the slightest venereal pleasure is serious matter. His final reason concerns the make-up of venereal pleasure. He says that no matter how light the pleasure is, the danger of proceeding and consenting to greater pleasure is always present. Lacroix does not believe that in venereal pleasure one can prescribe the boundaries. One cannot, he says, intend only so much venereal pleasure. Following the "co-cause" theory of Cardenas, Lacroix states that as soon as the cause which moves to arousal is present, there is immediately another cause which moves to seeking greater pleasure. Thus, according to Lacroix, anyone who desires slight venereal pleasure implicitly desires serious pleasure.[45]

Lacroix's adherence to the teaching of no parvity of matter was not as rigid as that of some of his predecessors. The probability of the parvity of matter opinion is not completely ruled out. Lacroix states that according to the tenth General of the Society of Jesus, Goswin Nickel (1652-1664) a Jesuit may absolve one who holds parvity of matter because he feels that the Holy See, according to theologians, had not yet officially denied the probability of the position.[46]

Lacroix says that one can admit parvity of matter in sexual matter if one is speaking in generic terms, for example, something common to both sensual and venereal pleasure. However, if one is speaking in specific terms, that is, of venereal pleasure, Lacroix says that there is no parvity of matter.[47] Kisses, touches, and looks are serious matter if done for the desire of venereal pleasure. If done out of custom, even if venereal pleasure arises, there is only light matter. He says that if such actions are performed out of jest or curiosity, the matter should also be considered light.[48]

With the arrival on the scene of Charles-Rene' Billuart, O.P. (1685-1757) a new distinction came into play -- the distinction between direct and indirect pleasure. It was a very important contribution to the question and one that most traditional theologians still use today.

Billuart readily admits that fact of venial sin in this area of the sixth and ninth commandments either because of lack of consent or sufficient reflection. But whether or not in these sins there is parvity of matter is a source of controversy among theologians. Billuart believes that most agree on the basics, but differ in the manner of expressing themselves.[49]

Lust is defined by Billuart as an inordinate appetite for venereal pleasure. It is a mortal sin <u>ex genere suo</u>.[50] Billuart asks the question, "Can there be parvity of matter in sins of lust?" Before answering the question, he distinguishes between sensual pleasure and venereal pleasure. Billuart makes no distinction between sensual and sensible pleasure. Sensual pleasure is that which arises when there is proportionality between a sensible object and its proper sense. Venereal pleasure is that which arises from genital excitation. According to Billuart there is parvity of matter in sensual pleasure. He states that there is sinful matter in sensual pleasure because the pleasure is desired for itself. In his opinion, there is a disorientation here.[51]

In discussing whether or not there can be parvity of matter in venereal pleasure, Billuart introduces the distinction between what is directly voluntary and indirectly voluntary. According to Billuart venereal pleasure is directly voluntary when it is sought in itself. It is indirectly voluntary when the pleasure is not sought in itself, but is foreseen, though not intended, as forthcoming because of its inseparable connection with some act. He says that in directly desired venereal pleasure, there is no parvity of matter. Billuart states that most theologians agree on this point. In his mind, even those who seem to hold the contrary opinion really agree with him. He says that when these adversaries talk about directly voluntary they actually mean indirectly voluntary.[52]

Billuart cites two reasons why there can be no parvity of matter in the sixth and ninth commandments. The first reason he gives is not staunchly defended by him. He just presents the argument and lets it stand on its own merits. According to Billuart certain actions in themselves are proximately light matter, but remotely and indirectly move toward serious matter. Such actions are not serious because they cause only a slight venereal arousal. However, he goes on to say that, even though these actions are in themselves light, still any action in this area is the beginning of the completed act. Thus Billuart concludes that there can be no light matter in directly desired venereal pleasure because every act in this area is ordered toward the completed act. As stated above, Billuart considered this first argument somewhat weak because it does not allow for acts of kissing and touching done out of levity or jokingly. According to the first argument, such actions do not admit of parvity of matter.[53] Billuart says that his second argument is a much more convincing one in denying parvity of matter in directly desired venereal pleasure. He states that man's nature is fragile as a result of original sin. Thus, it is not possible for one to consent to a slight venereal pleasure without proceeding to more serious matter. With this as a stated premise Billuart concludes that even in slight venereal pleasure the matter is serious because of the proximate danger of progressing to more serious matter.[54]

One might object to Billuart's last argument by stating

that among the married there is parvity of matter in directly willed venereal pleasure. Billuart agrees that this is true, but he denies the comparison. Among the married there is no danger of falling into further more serious acts, since such acts are permitted by reason of the married state. He also gives this as the reason why there can be parvity of matter in the other commandments. The danger of progressing to further and more serious acts is not present in those other commandments.[55]

Billuart admits the existence of parvity of matter in indirectly willed venereal pleasure as long as the danger of consent is absent. He reasons that the consent to further pleasure is lacking in the indirectly willed venereal pleasure. The consent is only to the cause, not to the venereal pleasure. He says that this is widely taught doctrine. According to Billuart, those who teach no parvity of matter are actually referring only to directly willed venereal pleasure. He cites the theologians of the Society of Jesus. He points out that they are forbidden by law to teach parvity of matter in the sixth and ninth commandments. Nevertheless, they teach that to kiss, to touch, or to view some nonstimulating parts of the body either out of levity or jokingly from which some venereal pleasure arises are at the most venial matter.[56]

One could object, Billuart says, that even in light matter the beginning of an orgasm is in process, and thereby serious matter. Billuart responds that the beginning of such a pollution is so far removed from its completed state as to be only a venial sin. He compares the gravity of the matter here to the quarrel that results in a homicide or the light drinking that results in drunkenness. Such actions are so far removed from the final stage that one could scarcely call them anything but venial sins. The same argument holds true for the slight venereal pleasure which is willed indirectly. He says that even though the disposition towards the completed act is present, to which it is ordered by its very nature, still this disposition is so far removed from the complete actuation stage that it can in no way be considered serious matter. Otherwise every occasion of sin would be considered serious matter. He strengthens his argument by appealing to pastoral practice. If every action which causes light venereal matter is a mortal sin, then many acts of conversation between men and women, between young men and young girls, kisses, touches and the like would have to be avoided since, for the most part, these actions give rise to slight venereal pleasure. Billuart says that no theologians hold this rigorous doctrine, as long as the danger of consent is not present. He goes on also to say that it is not the practice in the confessional.[57]

Billuart believes that kisses, touches, and looks, done only for sensual pleasure, are not serious sins. However, he does consider such actions dangerous, since in his mind it is easy to progress from sensual pleasure to venereal pleasure. The above-mentioned actions performed out of levity, out of curiosity or jokingly are only venial sins. To touch unnecessarily or kiss the intimate parts of another person's body is a serious sin.[58]

Alphonse Liguori (1696-1787) did not add much to the development of the argument. By his time the doctrine of no parvity of matter seems to have been solidly established among theologians. He does, however, add his weight to the doctrine as well as broadening its base to include sensible pleasure.

Liguori distinguishes between the two types of pleasures — venereal and sensible. He defines venereal pleasure as that pleasure which arises from the excitement of the genital organs. He considers sensible pleasure likewise as natural pleasure. It results from some proportion between the sense and its proper object.[59] He cites as examples of sensible pleasure the touch of a woman's hand, the touch of soft objects, and the smell of a rose.[60]

Before responding to the question concerning parvity of matter in venereal pleasure, Liguori cites a number of earlier theologians who hold parvity of matter. He lists Thomas Sanchez, Martinus of Azpilcueta (Doctor Navarrus), Dominic Soto, Juan de Salas and many Salamanca theologians as teaching parvity of matter in venereal pleasure as long as there is no danger of pollution or consent to a carnal act. He also lists Thomas Tamburinus who holds parvity of matter in sins of lust. However, Tamburinus includes sensible pleasure under the generic term of lust. He does not admit of parvity of matter in venereal pleasure.

Notwithstanding the authority of the above-mentioned theologians, Liguori follows the accepted teaching on the question. He does not admit of parvity of matter in venereal pleasure. He cites the condemnations of proposition 40 in 1666 by Pope Alexander VII as his reason.[61] Liguori states that if kissing for the purpose of venereal pleasure is grave matter, the same holds for the other acts of touch. He reasons that in any degree of venereal pleasure the completed act is already in motion or is in the process of becoming.[62]

Even in sensual pleasure Liguori does not admit parvity of matter. He cites Thomas Cajetan, Antonius Diana, and some Salamanca theologians as holding no parvity of matter even in this area. In his opinion the pleasure which arises from sensual acts is of itself directed towards pollution. It is not possible to enjoy sensual pleasure without experiencing venereal pleasure. He attributes this to our weak human nature wounded by original sin. This tendency is especially true for those who have reached puberty.

Theoretically, Liguori admits the possibility of an individual who through long experience could be morally certain that he would be immune to the danger of consenting to the venereal pleasure which accompanies sensual pleasure. Such a person would be very rare. However, the possibility exists in theory at least. If such an individual could perform an act in which the pleasure is purely sensual and does not perform the act for the pleasure, then Liguori admits the possibility of parvity of matter. Liguori sees the pleasure as just accompanying the act. On the other hand, if one performs the act for the pleasure, one cannot, in Liguori's opinion, separate himself from the danger of progressing into venereal pleasure.[63]

According to Liguori, kissing, embracing, and handshaking are ordinarily not sinful, if they are customary ways of showing friendship, even if venereal pleasure should arise. Of course, the presumption is that there is no consent given to the pleasure. He says, however, that even kisses which are the result of custom can be serious matter if they are prolonged and ardent. Liguori agrees with Thomas Sanchez who taught that kissing between two adolescents is ordinarily a venial sin because the pleasure that arises from such acts is usually sensual.[64] The same holds true for that pleasure which arises from horseplay, levity, and curiosity as long as all venereal pleasure is absent.[65] Liguori says that to touch oneself from levity or out of curiosity is not serious matter as long as there is a just cause for the action and no venereal pleasure.[66] To touch another is a serious sin unless necessity demands such an action. But if done accidentally out of jest or curiosity, there is no serious matter present. Liguori, however, agrees with Salamanca theologians who question the meaning of "light touch." They consider that such an action exists only in the speculative order and not in the practical.[67] To look at the bust, arms, or legs of another person's body briefly is not serious matter according to Liguori, provided there is no danger of sinning seriously. He cites Doctor Navarrus, Thomas Sanchez, Cajetan and the Salamanca theologians as holding this position.[68]

In summary, one can see in this chapter that the formation of the teaching of no parvity of matter in the sixth and ninth commandments developed over a period of time. The interesting part of this development was not the actual question itself. There was little controversy in this area. The no parvity of matter doctrine was almost universally accepted from the very beginning. The development centered more on the proper understanding of the term and the reasons for the no parvity of matter teaching.

St. Thomas's thought on the question evolved. In his earlier writings he denied the existence of parvity of matter in all sins mortal ex genere suo.[69] He later rethought his position and allowed for parvity of matter in this category of sins which admit of parvity of matter, he made no mention of sins of lust in this area.[70] One can legitimately conclude from this deliberate omission that St. Thomas considers all sins of this type to be serious matter.

In Martinus Magister the pendulum swings to the opposite extreme. He takes issue with St. Thomas's definition of libidinous acts and seemingly teaches the legitimacy of deliberately seeking venereal pleasure under certain conditions.[71] In all fairness to Martinus, we should point out that theologians question his own understanding of libidinous acts and his teaching on venereal pleasure. However, if taken at face value, his extremely liberal position breaks not only with St. Thomas, but with all previous teaching on the subject.

Thomas Sanchez was another theologian whose thoughts on parvity of matter went through a process of evolution. He was a rigorist in the beginning, but as time went on he admitted parvity of matter in the sixth and ninth commandments. He was one of the first to view the seriousness of matter qua matter apart from the adjoining circumstances. In other words, the matter of sexual acts was serious notwithstanding the possibility of consent to venereal pleasure or of proceeding to further sins. Even though Sanchez continually referred to parvity of matter in venereal pleasure, nevertheless he so identified the pleasure and the act which produces the pleasure that in reality he held parvity of acts. In his mind a light sexual touch causes only a slight amount of venereal pleasure. Thus the parvity of matter is present not by reason of the slight pleasure, but rather because of the light sexual touch.[72]

The decree of Claude Acquaviva almost terminated all free discussion on parvity of matter. Jesuits who were very influential in the field of education were forbidden to teach parvity of matter. Thus, from the time of the proclamation of the decree the discussion for the most part was one-sided. The theological reasons in support of the no parvity of matter were discussed and developed. In all fairness to Acquaviva, however, one has to say the past was in his favor. Tradition and the greater majority of theologians with few exceptions taught the no parvity of matter doctrine. Consequently, we can say that, even though the decree might have been the result of a general laxist tendency among Jesuits, it really did not stop discussion of the question but rather pushed it in a certain direction.

Though the decree stopped Jesuit theologians from arguing for the existence of parvity of matter, other theologians continued the discussion. Juan Caramuel introduced the distinction in this matter between the speculative and the practical orders. He sees no reason why parvity of matter cannot exist in the speculative order. The light touch of another person's hand or the fleeting glance at the face of a beautiful woman certainly cannot be serious matter according to Caramuel. However, since those acts expose a person to the possibility of seeking greater satisfaction, in practice there can be no parvity of matter.

As might be expected, John Cardenas, S.J. taught the no parvity of matter doctrine. Much of his writing in this area is devoted to answering the criticism of Caramuel against the Society and developing reasons in support of the no parvity of matter teaching. Cardenas centers his reasons for his position around man's limitations. The weakness of one's will to control its appetite or the inability of one's intellect to resolve a practical doubt really account for the impossibility of parvity of matter. The lightness or seriousness of the matter itself is not considered.

Claudius Lacroix, S.J. was another defender of the no parvity of matter teaching. He introduced a new dimension to the argument. He writes that all venereal pleasure is ordered to the completed act, and for that reason even the slightest amount of pleasure is serious matter.

The Dominican Charles-Rene' Billuart combines the arguments of Lacroix and Cardenas. He gives as reasons against the parvity of matter teaching that man is so weak and fragile because of original sin that one cannot be satisfied with a slight venereal pleasure. He also cites the fact that the acts which produce venereal pleasure have an innate tendency to reach out towards the completed act. Because of his distinction between directly and indirectly willed venereal pleasure, he was able to admit parvity of matter under certain conditions.

Alphonsus Liguori was quite rigid in his teaching of no parvity of matter. He readily admits the teaching in reference to venereal pleasure because in his mind even the slightest pleasure is in process to becoming the completed act. His contribution to the question could be considered negative in the sense that he extended the no parvity of matter even to sensual pleasure. In his mind this pleasure and venereal pleasure go hand in hand. The former always includes the latter. Speculatively, one could say the possibility of enjoying purely sensual pleasure really exists; however, in practice it rarely happens because of man's weak nature.

1 Karl-Heinz Kleber, <u>De Parvitate Materiae in Sexto</u>, Studien zur Geschichte der Kath. Moral-theologie, Heraus-gegeban von Michael Muller no. 18 (Regensburg: Verlag Friedrick Pustet, 1971), p. 98.

2 St. Thomas Aquinas, <u>Scriptum Super Libros Sententiarum</u>, Lib.II, Distinctio XXIV, Quaestio III, Articulus IV.

3 St. Thomas Aquinas, <u>Summa Theologica</u>, II-II, 118, 4.

4 Ibid., 66, 6, ad 3.

5 "It should nevertheless be considered that in some genera of mortal sin one can find an act which is not mortal because of its own imperfection, namely it does not possess all that is necessary for its completeness. This can happen in one of two ways. In the first instance, an agent can perform an act which does not proceed from his full deliberateness. Such deliberation is an essential aspect for the positing of a human act. An example of this occurs when one has a sudden impulse to murder or commit adultery. These acts are not considered mortal sins because they do not proceed from man's reason, which they must if an act is to attain its completeness. In the second instance, an act in the genera of mortal sin can be prevented from being a mortal sin because of the moral object itself. An act in the genera of mortal sin is not serious if the matter is small because reason considers small matter as nothing. This can happen in sins of theft." St. Thomas Aquinas, <u>De Malo</u>, Quaestio X, Articulus II.

6 "Accordingly, therefore, it can happen that, even though the sin of envy is in the genus of mortal sin, every sin of envy is not necessarily a mortal sin, mainly because the act does not reach its completeness..... Such as happens when an individual is dejected over some other's good which is so small that it appears to be bereft of all desirability." Ibid, Quaestio X, Articulus II.

7 "Another way an act can lack its completeness is because of the matter, which can be so insignificant that it is almost nothing..... Venial sin can occur in sins of anger in both way -- in the one instance when a sudden impulse to become angry occurs, but to which the reason does not concur, and in the second instance when the injury is small." Ibid, Quaestio XII, Articulus II.

8 "If indeed greediness is generally called an inordinate love or desire of the things of this world, then greediness is not always a mortal sin." Ibid, Quaestio XIII, Articulus II.

9 "And, therefore, the disorder concerning the emission of semen centers around the coming into being of person in proximate potency. Hence, it is obvious that all such acts of lust are mortal sins of their very nature." Ibid, Quaestio XV, Articulus II.

10 "In reply to the eighteenth objection, it should be said that touches, embraces, and kisses insofar as they are ordered to the act of fornication follow one's consent; insofar as they are ordered to the pleasure only follow upon one's consent to the pleasure which is a mortal sin. For that reason in both instances the sins are mortal." Ibid, Quaestio XV, Articulus II, ad 18.

11 "But pleasure in the act of fornication itself is a mortal sin in its very genus. The fact that it can be a venial sin before the consent is given is only per accidens, namely because of the incompleteness of the act. However, this incompleteness ceases when the act proceeds from deliberate consent." St. Thomas Aquinas, Summa Theologica, I-II, 74, 8, ad 2.

12 Martinus Magister, Quaestiones morales. Tom. 1 (De Temperantia cum virtutibus adnexis), Parisiis, 1490, fol. 64, as quoted in Karl-Heinz Kleber, De Parvitate Materiae in Sexto, pp. 102-103.

13 Kleber, op. cit., p. 103.

14 Ibid.

15 Martinus Magister, Quaestiones morales, fol. 65., as quoted in Karl-Heinz Kleber p. 104.

16 ".....it seems that venereal pleasure which if the result of thoughts alone or from touches admits of smallness of matter." Doctor Navarrus, Opera Omnia: Commentarius in septem distinctiones de poenitentia, Distinctio prima; caput "Si Cui" nr. 17, p. 246.

17 Charles E. Curran, Contemporary Problems in Moral Theology, (Notre Dame: Fides Publishers, Inc., 1970), p. 164.

18 Doctor Navarrus, Opera Omnia, op. cit.

19 Thomas Sanchez, Opus morale, par. 2, lib. 5, cap. 6, nr. 13., and De Matrimonio, lib. 9, nr. 5, p. 312.

20 Thomas Sanchez, De Matrimonio, lib. 9, disp. 46, nr. 16, p. 314.

21 Ibid.

22 Ibid.

23 Ibid, nr. 12, p. 315.

24 Ibid, nr. 25, p. 315.

25 Karl-Heinz Kleber, De Parvitate Materiae in Sexto, op. cit., p. 123.

26 Thomas Sanchez, S.J., Opus Morale, pars. 2, lib. 5, cap. 12, p. 45.

27 R. Brouillard, "Sanchez, Thomas" in DTC, Vol. 14, (Librairie Letouzey et Ane, Paris, 1939), 1078-1079.

28 Ordinationes et Selectae Epistolae Praepositi Generalis Societatis Jesu, Epp. NN. 115, p. 498, unpublished collection located in the Archivum Romanum Societatis Jesu, Romae, Borgo S. Spirito, C.P. 9048. Quoted in Karl-Heinz Kleber, De Parvitate Materiae in Sexto, pp. 172-174.

29 Ibid.

30 Ibid.

31 Ibid., Epp. NN 113, p. 260.

32 Ibid., Epp. NN 115, p. 498.

33 Ibid., Ponte Jesuitico 657, p. 425.

34 Juan Caramuel (de Lobkowitz), Commentarius in Regulam D. Benedicti, disp. 69, nr. 1052, p. 418.

35 "I measure the gravity of the fault from the quantity of the pleasure and so I philosophise from my own principles. That pleasure which is the result of more than one-eighth of the emission is serious and mortally sinful. Any thing less than an eighth is light matter. It is obvious from my principles which I have so effectively demonstrated above that an eighth part of an orgasm is the smallest matter of a grave sin. Thus, the pleasure which is less than an eighth part of the orgasm (unless another occasion of sin presents itself) will be a venial fault." Ibid, nr. 1055, p. 421.

36 Juan Caramuel (de Lobkowitz) Theologia Moralis Fundamentalis, lib. 2, fundament. 57, nr. 2716, p. 860.

37 Ibid., nr. 2764, p. 877.

38 Ibid., nr. 2709, p. 861.

39 Ibid., nr. 2710, p. 861.

40 John Cardenas, S.J., <u>Crisis Theologica</u>, Venice, 1710, tract 5, disp. 45, cap. 4, nr. 30, p. 364.

41 Ibid., nr. 1, p. 361.

42 Ibid., cap. 8, nr. 97, p. 368.

43 Ibid., nr. 108, p. 369.

44 Ibid., nr. 116, p. 369.

45 Claudius Lacroix, S.J., <u>Theologia Moralis</u>, Tom. 1, lib. 3, pars. 1, cap. 2, dub. 1, Quaestio 196, nr. 910, pp. 285-286.

46 Ibid., Quaestio 196, nr. 911, p. 286.

47 Ibid., nr. 912, p. 286.

48 Ibid., Tom. 1, lib. 3, pars. 1, cap. 2, dub. 1, nr. 887, p. 216.

49 Charles-Rene' Billuart, O.P., <u>Summa S. Thomae hodiernis academiarum moribus accomodata cursus theologiae universalis</u>, Wirceburgii, 1758, Tom. 2, tract de Temperantia, diss. 5, art. 1, nota, p. 830.

50 Ibid., art. 1, p. 829

51 Ibid., art. 2, p. 830.

52 Ibid.

53 Ibid.

54 Ibid.

55 Ibid., p. 831.

56 Ibid.

57 Ibid.

58 Ibid., p. 867.

59 Alphonsus Liguori, C.SS.R., <u>Theologia Moralis</u>, Antwerps, 1821, Tom. II, lib. 3, tract. IV, Cap. 2, nr. 415, p. 284.

60 Ibid., nr. 416, p. 286.

61 Denziger, H. and Schoenmetzer, A., Enchiridion Symbolorum (Frieburg: Herder, 1962), No. 2060. "It is a probable opinion, which states that a kiss, indulged in for carnal and sensible pleasure which arises from it is only light matter, provided that there is no danger of further consent and pollution."

62 Liguori, <u>Theologia Moralis</u>, nr. 415, pp. 284-285.

63 Ibid., nr. 416, pp. 286-287.

64 Ibid., nr. 417, p. 287.

65 Ibid., nr. 418, p. 287.

66 Ibid., nr. 419, p. 287.

67 Ibid., nr. 420, pp. 288-290.

68 Ibid., nr. 423, p. 291.

69 St. Thomas Aquinas, <u>Scriptum Super Libros Sententiarum</u>, Lib. II., Distinctio XXIV, Quaestio III, Articulus IV.

70 St. Thomas Aquinas, <u>De Malo</u>, Quaestio XII, Articulus III and Quaestio XIII, Articulus II.

71 Martinus Magister, <u>Quaestiones morales</u>, Tom. 1 (De temperantia cum virtutibus adnexis), (Paris, 1490), fol. 64.

72 "One may question whether these light touches, indulged in for pleasure, are mortal sins.... for me it is very difficult to see how they are. Even though touches of a more serious nature can certainly be considered the beginning of intercourse because the pleasure, which arises from them, pushes one more vehemently to intercourse, still light touches contain such little evil that they are excused from being mortal because of the smallness of the matter, even if the pleasure is directly sought. The pleasure is too slight to constitute a mortal sin." Thomas Sanchez, S.J., <u>De sancto matrimonii sacramento disputationum</u>, (Venice, 1606), lib. 9, disp 46, nr. 16, p. 314.

Chapter II

The Teaching of the Approved Authors Prior to Vatican II

By the middle of the eighteenth century the teaching of no parvity of matter in sins against the sixth and ninth commandments was firmly established and the theological reasons fairly well developed. An over-protective magisterium and the natural law approach to moral theology left little room for discussion in this area. This traditional teaching of theologians from 1750 to the time just prior to Vatican II was reflected in the manualists of the first half of the twentieth century. In this chapter we will look at some of these prominent theologians and their teaching on parvity of matter. This will give us some idea of the status of the teaching and the supporting arguments prior to the time it was challenged and how it developed over the years.

Edward Genicot, S.J. was one of the earliest manualists who taught the traditional doctrine on parvity of matter. His thoughts and reasoning on the matter do not differ much from his predecessors. In fact, he relies heavily on the doctrine of St. Alphonsus Liguori. His teaching on the morality of kisses, embraces, hand-holding, and similar acts is the same as Liguori's. Thus, it is not surprising that Genicot follows the traditional line when writing about the gravity of complete and incomplete venereal acts.[1]

Genicot defines the act of "pollution" as complete venereal satisfaction by some form of stimulation. Such an act is an intrinsically serious evil. Hence he allows for no parvity of matter in such acts. He reasons that nature intended the propagation of the human race through the fertilization by the man's seed with the egg in the womb of a woman. In the case of "pollution" as he describes it, viz., male masturbation, obviously this is not possible. The end of the act is thwarted because the human seed is posited outside the vagina. The malice of the act consists in the fact that the order by which nature intends to stabilize the conservation of the human race is overturned. Secondly, the stability of the marriage state would be seriously jeopardized, if the unmarried could legitimately indulge in acts of complete sexual actuation and the accompanying venereal pleasure. In Genicot's opinion fewer and fewer men and women would feel the need to marry. The burdens of married life and the enjoyment of venereal pleasure go hand in hand.[2]

After stating that there is no parvity of matter in acts of complete sexual actuation, Genicot turns his attention to the gravity of incomplete sexual acts. The matter is always serious. Anyone who directly seeks venereal pleasure in any degree sins gravely. Grave sin is also present for one who voluntarily delights in such pleasure which might arise spontaneously. Thus, Genicot is definitely in the tradition of Jesuit moralists since the time of Acquaviva's decree and most theologians since 1750. In his opinion there is no parvity of matter in directly willed acts against the sixth and ninth commandments.[3]

Genicot bases his argument for his no parvity of matter doctrine on the nature of venereal pleasure. He states that it is very difficult to place limits on the enjoyment of venereal pleasure. No matter how slight the pleasure there always seems to be the desire to seek more. When one directly seeks and desires a slight venereal pleasure, one exposes himself to the obvious danger of consenting to a greater pleasure and manifestly more seriously sinful. Genicot believes that the same danger is present in venereal pleasure that arises spontaneously. In his mind the transit from this involuntary to the voluntary state can occur very easily.[4]

In support of this teaching, Genicot appeals to external arguments. He cites the decree of Alexander VII in which proposition 40 of the moral laxists was condemned. This proposition stated that one could directly seek and enjoy delectationem carnalem et sensibilem which arises from a kiss as long as the danger of pollution and further sinful acts were absent. Although Genicot readily admits that the condemnation of the proposition does not directly rule out the possibility of parvity of matter, he feels that the condemnation of parvity of matter is still there at least implicitly. In the light of the proposition, he believes that it would be very difficult to hold parvity of matter.[5]

However, Genicot does not rely too heavily on the Alexander VII condemnation of proposition 40. He admits there there is some confusion in the minds of theologians concerning the precise meaning of the proposition. Some are in doubt as to the meaning of the word "carnalem". It is synonymous with "sensibilem" or does it mean venereal? Domenico Viva states that in the context "carnalem" and venereal have the same meaning. Other theologians question the quality of the acts in the proposition. They feel that the real sense of the proposition refers to those acts which by nature proximately dispose one to venereal pleasure and venereal excitement. In their thinking the proposition does not extend itself to include light and fleeting kisses.[6]

H. Noldin, S.J. and A. Schmitt, S.J., were prominent theologians who taught in the Gregorian University in Rome. Since they were Jesuits, it is not surprising that they held to the traditional teaching of parvity of matter. They state the general principle that the evil of sins of lust consists in the fact that God intended man to enjoy venereal pleasure only in marriage and according to the laws of marriage. Venereal pleasure is ordered toward propagation because the act from which it draws its morality is ordered to the same end. To enjoy or seek venereal pleasure outside marriage or within marriage but not according to the laws of marriage is an abuse.[7]

Noldin and Schmitt say that directly willed venereal pleasure outside of marriage is serious matter. They cite four reasons in support of this statement. The enjoyment of venereal pleasure illicitly is against the order of nature. All venereal experience is ordered to one specific act, namely that act which promotes generation. This unique act is the conjugal act, exercised properly only in marriage. In their second reason the authors discuss the proper end of the act. It is a great disorder to subject something which is intended for the good of the species and for the propagation of the human race to one's own private convenience. This is precisely what happens when one seeks venereal pleasure outside the marriage state. It is subordinating one's reason in a matter of the greatest importance. Thirdly, the seeking of venereal pleasure outside marriage would cause very great harm to the human race. Men and women would avoid the burden of the marital state if they could enjoy venereal pleasure free from all moral sanctions. Such a situation would be greatly detrimental to the human race and would greatly hinder its propagation. Their final argument in support of the seriousness of sins in this area is taken from Scripture. God has prohibited all kinds of sins of impurity. They cite the writings of St. Paul in which he enumerates those sins of impurity which exclude one from the kingdom of God.[8]

After discussing the malice of sins of lust, Noldin and Schmitt turn their attention to the question of degrees of malice. In sins against the sixth and ninth commandments, they state that there is no light matter. The relationship of venereal pleasure to the propagation of the human race does not allow for degrees of malice. No matter how scant or how brief the enjoyment of the venereal pleasure is, the matter of the sin is always serious. In their minds that total disorder which occurs in the exercise of the generative faculty outside of marriage is present in any degree of venereal pleasure. Thus, even the slightest venereal pleasure is ordered to the good of the species, namely its propagation. They add another reason for holding their opinion. In their minds a set-degree of venereal pleasure is an impossibility. Any degree of venereal pleasure directly willed or freely accepted, no matter how slight, exposes one to the danger of further sin. This type of pleasure of its nature compels one to seek the complete pleasure. Because of these reasons Noldin and Schmitt conclude that any venereal pleasure even though slight and brief is serious matter. If the other elements for sin are present -- free consent and sufficient reflection -- they state that a serious sin is committed.[9]

Noldin and Schmitt argue that the sixth and ninth commandments are somewhat unique among the ten commandments in not allowing parvity of matter, whereas the majority of the other commandments allow for degrees of seriousness. They cite two reasons for this. In sins, for example, against the majority of the other commandments the matter is able to be light since the total disorder is not fully present in each degree as it is in venereal pleasure. In their second reason for this uniqueness of the sixth and ninth commandments in this matter they state that the inclination to further acts of sin is not present in sins against the other commandments as it is in the sixth and ninth.[10]

The authors reject the argument of those who say that venereal pleasure is the beginning of pollution. According to these theologians, even the slightest degree of venereal pleasure is the product of genital excitation. They argue that such excitation naturally causes pollution. Nolding and Schmitt deny the universal applicability of this theory. They say there are those who can experience venereal pleasure without it being the beginning of an orgasm. They cite pre-pubescent youths and eunuchs as examples. These can experience venereal pleasure without it being the beginning of orgasm since they are unable to produce sperm.[11]

Nolding and Schmitt state there was a time when a few theologians held parvity of matter in venereal pleasure. However, since 1612, when Claude Acquaviva forbade all Jesuits from teaching parvity of matter in any form, the no parvity of matter doctrine became almost universally accepted. To those who say that the arguments in favor of parvity of matter have validity in the speculative order, Noldin and Schmitt respond that in the speculative order their arguments show the parvity of matter view to be false and nonprobable, in the practical order the arguments prove the doctrine to be certainly false and less safe.[12]

In his work, <u>Moral and Pastoral Theology</u>, Henry Davis, S.J., proposes two arguments in favor of the no parvity of matter teaching. The first argument states that even the smallest degree of incomplete pleasure has reference by its very nature to the conjugal act and to that alone. It is a perversion of nature to procure or accept that pleasure without reference to the end of the conjugal act. Venereal pleasure was given to mankind by God so that man and woman could be attracted in marriage to the mutual office of propagating the human race. In arousing desire for this pleasure the individual must recognize that this capability is his only insofar as it is subordinated to the good of the species. Davis says all moral theologians hold this doctrine of no parvity of matter in sexual sins. He believes that the discussion is closed both because of the intrinsic arguments and because of the unanimous agreement of theologians. In his mind no theologian would venture to call it in question.[13]

Davis's second argument in support of the no parvity of matter teaching is similar to the first. It centers around the nature of the act. Every venereal movement has an essential relation to the conjugal act, which is to be exercised only in marriage. Notwithstanding the objection of Noldin and Schmitt concerning the inability of pre-pubescent youths and eunuchs to experience orgasms, every venereal movement according to Davis is the natural beginning of and preparation for the complete conjugal act. All venereal pleasure which is sought outside marriage destroys that relationship and transfers what is meant for the good of the species to the "good" of the individual. He states that such a transference is intrinsically and seriously evil because it is the inversion of an essential order intended by nature. Any individual who seeks or accepts venereal pleasure is exercising an act which should be exercised on behalf of the species. He violates the subordination to the species which he should maintain. The relationship that one has to the preservation of the race is absolutely necessary and essential to the preservation of the species. In Davis's mind an order is established between the individual and the species. Thus, he concludes that this order and relationship are completely destroyed by every act of seeking or accepting venereal pleasure outside the marriage state.[14] Davis would also agree that this same disorder occurs within the marriage state whenever a married couple engage in contraceptive intercourse or have an induced or provoked orgasm apart from intercourse.

After determining the essential relationship that exists between venereal pleasure and the preservation of the species, Davis says there is no need to consider degrees of seriousness of these acts, if indeed these acts destroy that essential and necessary relationship. According to his reasoning each act is a grievous disorder. The same does not hold for the other virtues. Slight violations against charity, or obedience, or justice leave these virtues substantially intact. However, he states that in every act of venereal pleasure outside of marriage, there is a complete inversion of an essential and necessary order. Thus, there is no room for parvity of matter. Davis agrees with those who say that lying is opposed to the order of society, yet admits of degrees. Nevertheless, he denies the similarity. The difference consists in the fact that sins of unchastity are subversive of the very structure of society, whereas society can endure in spite of lying. Truthfulness does not preserve the human race, but the generation of offspring does.[15]

To bolster his argument in support of the no parvity of matter doctrine, Davis turns to papal documents. He first cites the response of the Holy Office. In 1661, the question was asked whether or not a confessor who is guilty of solicitation should be denounced even when the matter is slight. The Holy Office responded that in matters of impurity there is no parvity of matter.[16] Davis also notes that Popes Clement VIII and Paul V ordered those be denounced who hold that kissing, embracing, and touching for venereal pleasure are not grievous sins. He further cites Pope Alexander VII's condemnation of proposition 40. From these condemnations Davis states that one has to admit that all incomplete venereal pleasure directly willed outside the marriage state is a grievous sin because in the moral sphere the pleasure is not less venereal because it is slight. In the case of theft, Davis admits that there can be a greater or lesser act of injustice. However, this is not so when dealing with acts involving venereal pleasure. No matter how slight or how great the pleasure, the disorder is always the same; that is, it is detrimental to the preservation of the species and precisely in the same way.[17]

From the above evidence Davis draws two conclusions. The first is that it is grievously sinful for one deliberately to procure or to accept even the smallest degree of venereal pleasure outside marriage. His second conclusion is that it is equally sinful to think, to say, or to do anything with the intention of arousing even the smallest degree of pleasure.[18]

Davis states these same two conclusions in another way. One could object that one cannot possibly know when the smallest degree of venereal pleasure is present. Thus, according to the objection there can be no question of formal sin because of lack of advertence on the part of the one performing the act. The objection also states that the beginning of venereal pleasure, if very slight, defies analysis. Hence, again, there can be no formal sin. In response to these objections, Davis merely rephrases his two conclusions. If, in fact, venereal pleasure arises, no matter how slight, then there exists matter for grievous sin in the unmarried. The same hold true for those who are married if their enjoyment of venereal pleasure leads to masturbation. If the unmarried deliberately provoke such a pleasure, a grievous sin is committed at least materially. Davis summarizes the above by saying that in the matter of venereal pleasure there is no venial or morally slight amount.[19]

Before concluding this matter, Davis discussed the uniqueness of the no parvity of matter teaching. He restates the reasons why there is no room for light matter in sins against the sixth and ninth commandments. In his opinion the consequences of indulging in incomplete venereal pleasure are detrimental to the human race. On rational grounds alone one is forced to conclude that this abuse of a natural function is a serious disorder, since the effect of it is so dreadful and inevitable. The smallest amount of venereal pleasure is an inducement to indulge in it to the fullest. If a small amount of deliberate venereal pleasure were permitted to those not married, the human race would suffer grievous harm. No ordinary person can settle for a modicum of venereal pleasure. In enjoying even the smallest degree of this pleasure one exposes himself to actual orgasm and according to Davis this orgasm would be realized. He concludes his argument on the question of no parvity of matter by saying that it is the opinion of all theologians and is Catholic teaching that from the first beginning of venereal pleasure through its progressive stages to the complete actuation, there is at every point matter of serious disorder and grievous sin for those who are not married.[20]

Just as the decree of Claude Acquaviva had great influence on the teachings of Jesuits in the nineteenth and twentieth centuries, so it is not surprising that theologians outside the Society felt the influence of their predecessors in this matter. Thus it was for J. Aertnys and C. A. Damen. These men were respected moral theologians of the Redemptorist Congregation. As members of the same community as St. Alphonsus Liguori, they were greatly influenced by his thoughts and teachings in theology. After giving the traditional definition of lust and after making the standard distinctions between consummated and non-consummated acts, the authors take up the question of gravity of matter in sins of lust. They state the principle that all completed acts of lust which are direct and deliberate are mortal sins <u>ex toto genere suo</u>. Such acts do not allow for lightness of matter. This principle embraces not only consummated acts but all sexual pleasure outside of marriage.[21]

They support their argument, first of all, from Scripture. Ephesians 5:3-5 reads that every fornicator and impure person do not have heredity in the kingdom of Christ and God. In First Corinthians 6:9-10 St. Paul writes that no fornicator, nor adulterer, nor solitary sinners, nor prostitutes can possess the kingdom of God. As a final reference from Scripture, the authors refer the reader to Galatians 5:19-21.[22]

Aertnys and Damen use an argument from reason for the second proof of their position. Every misuse of acts venereal in nature of themselves harms the good of the human species. This misuse of these venereal acts deprives the generative faculty of its proper end, namely the propagation and rearing of offspring. Such a disorder is always a grievous sin because it is injurious to the greatest good of a potential human being, namely its coming into existence. In other words, the wrong use of the generative faculty deprives the human species of its basic and greatest good -- its propagation and proper upbringing.[23]

After treating the morality of completed acts of lust, Aertnys and Damen discuss those acts that do not reach their final stage of completion. They distinguish those incomplete acts of lust from merely sensual acts, such as kissing, embracing, and hand-holding. These acts are not venereal by nature but can lead to venereal acts.[24]

In discussing incomplete acts of lust, the authors state that any venereal enjoyment even light, directly willed or accepted, is always a grave sin. The argument used to support this statement is basically the same one as in support of the principle concerning the completed act. All acts of lust directly willed involve serious matter because every act of lust deprives the generative faculty of its proper end -- procreation and proper rearing of offspring.[25]

More specifically, Aertnys and Damen cite four arguments why there can be no parvity of matter in the incomplete act. First, the act of generation is forbidden sub gravi to all outside the marriage state. All genital excitation falls under the same interdict, since it uniquely looks towards the act of generation. Second, any genital excitation is in reality the beginning of orgasm, since of its nature it tends towards completion. Since all activity takes its species and its moral good or evil from its end, as a cause from its effect, genital excitation partakes of the same malice as an orgasm. Third, direct consent to light venereal pleasure necessarily generates the danger of consent to more serious acts. As a final argument, the authors cite the condemnation of proposition 40 by Alexander VII.[26]

Benedict H. Merkelbach, O.P., professor of moral theology at the Angelicum, follows the teaching of the other manualists. All sins of lust are serious matter ex toto genere suo. He cites Galatians, in which Paul says that lust is one of the works which excludes one from the kingdom of God. Secondly, sins of lust are grievous because by their very nature they exceed the order and proper balance of right reason. The use of acts venereal in nature is necessary for the common good, namely the preservation of the human race. These acts are as necessary for the preservation of the human race as food is necessary for the preservation of one's life. The more necessary something is, the more one must preserve the right order of reason. The misuse of acts venereal in nature violates this right order and is of itself serious matter.[27]

Merkelbach believes that sins of lust violate legal justice, God's dominion over man's body, and the right order of nature. As stated above, sins of this type harm the common good insofar as the propagation and conservation of the human race are necessary to preserve the common good. Any action which harms the common good violates the rights of those who are dependent on it. This is a violation of legal justice and therefore serious matter. Sins of lust usurp the right God has over our bodies. God is the principal lord of man's body. It is given to man only for his use and for a definite purpose. If through sins of lust one uses his body solely for his own pleasure, he thwarts God's purpose and calls into question God's dominion. Such sins constitute serious matter. Finally, in sins of lust the right order of nature is inverted. Nature intends the individual good of a person to be subordinated to the common good and the good of the species. In sins of lust the individual's good is put before all else. Thus the order intended by nature is inverted. These sins are serious matter.[28]

After discussing the gravity of sins of lust, Merkelbach turns his attention to degrees of seriousness. He states that venereal pleasure directly willed is a serious sin for the non-married ex toto genere suo. The matter in sins of lust admits of no degrees. In other words, all directly willed sins of lust, even to the slightest degree whether complete acts or not, are serious matter. There is no parvity of matter.[29]

Merkelbach cites three arguments in support of his position. All venereal pleasure no matter how slight is ordered by nature to the propagation of the human race within the marriage state. The misuse of this pleasure is opposed to the primary intention of nature and God. The second argument in favor of the no parvity of matter teaching is based on a principle of St. Thomas Aquinas. In the Summa St. Thomas writes that the beginning of anything is ordered to its completion. In other words, whoever begins anything, by the very fact of beginning implicitly and necessarily desires its completion, just as whoever wishes a participated good by that very fact reaches out towards the total good, because it is only the total good that will satisfy the individual.[30] Thus, it is in the enjoyment of light venereal pleasure according to Merkelbach. Incomplete venereal pleasure of its very nature tends toward the completed act because it is the actual beginning of that act. Hence, anyone who seeks incomplete or light venereal pleasure directly by that very fact loves and desires the completed act, not as a consequence, but as something to be desired Since complete venereal pleasure is serious matter for the non-married because it is directly opposed to the common good of the human species, so also is incomplete venereal pleasure serious matter because it is nothing other than the beginning of the complete pleasure.[31]

Merkelbach poses a possible objection to his above argument. Since the intellect is man's highest power and governs the extent of any human act, it would seem that one could abstract from complete pleasure through one's intellect and conclude to the possibility of parvity of matter. Merkelbach denies this possibility. He replies to the objection by saying that the beginning of the act is of its very nature ordered to the completed act. The abstraction of the intellect and the intention of the will can in no way change the nature of the act. In his mind the objection has no validity in this area. One cannot intend to exclude complete venereal pleasure and desire only incomplete venereal pleasure. Such a one acts against his own will. By desiring incomplete venereal pleasure one implicitly and necessarily seeks complete pleasure. The incomplete pleasure has no desirability unless as a beginning or a part of the complete pleasure and by reason of the complete pleasure.[32]

Merkelbach's third argument against parvity of matter centers around the proximate-occasion-of-sin theory. Anyone who directly wills venereal pleasure exposes himself to the grave danger of seeking further and complete venereal pleasure because of original sin. The vehemence of carnal concupiscence and common human weakness do not allow one to be satisfied with incomplete venereal pleasure. He concludes that it is impossible for anyone to seek incomplete venereal pleasure without implicitly seeking and desiring complete pleasure. He also concludes that it is impossible for anyone to seek incomplete venereal pleasure without the disposition toward the complete pleasure and exposing oneself to that danger. Merkelbach believes that this was precisely the point of the famous proposition 40, condemned by Alexander VII. In Merkelbach's opinion, those who taught this proposition supposed wrongly that a kiss, sought for venereal pleasure, does not lead one to the danger of further sins.[33]

These first two chapters showed not only the historical development of the parvity of matter teaching, but also the theological development. In the sixteenth and seventeenth centuries a certain amount of confusion and unclarity in the status of the question, in the terms, and in the substantiating arguments is evident. Theologians acknowledged the no parvity of matter teaching, but their reasons for their stand were varied and needed development. As time went on, the question became more defined and the arguments somewhat more developed until the time of the manualists of the twentieth century. These manualists presented a united front in support of the no parvity of matter doctrine. Unlike their predecessors they treated the question directly. The gravity of matter in sins against the sixth and ninth commandments was considered in itself and not because of some extrinsic circumstance which would "attribute" seriousness to the matter. In other words, the manualists, as it were, weighed the matter. They developed one main argument in favor of the traditional teaching which was intrinsic to the matter of sexual sins. This is not to say that they did not proffer other intrinsic arguments to bolster their position. They did. Genicot and Noldin, for example, state that the institution of marriage would be greatly jeopardized, if men and women could pursue venereal pleasure with impunity. They concluded, therefore, that the matter in such sins is always serious. However, other than their own main argument, the manualists never considered these other intrinsic arguments as very convincing or supportive of their position.

Like their predecessors the manualists had no problem in accepting the teaching of no parvity of matter. Three centuries of tradition supported their position. As was stated above, they were more concerned with identifying and determining the arguments in support of the teaching than with the fact itself. In their search for a convincing argument, the manualists looked to reason for their answer. They argued that the relationship between venereal pleasure and the finality of all genital excitation -- the propagation of the human species -- makes parvity of matter in sexual sins impossible. All venereal acts are ordered to this end. Because of the magnitude and importance of the propagation of the human species, any act which deviates from that end is serious matter. This gravity of matter extends itself not only to the act itself, but also to all the elements related to the act. This obviously would include all venereal pleasure. The manualists reasoned that venereal pleasure was as much related to the end of the generative act as the act itself. Thus they concluded that there can be no parvity of matter in sins against the sixth and ninth commandments.

The historical development of the parvity of matter question shows that the manualists relied mainly on arguments from reason to support their position. A perusal of the literature shows that the official magisterium of the Church had little to say about parvity of matter. In fact, one finds the magisterium almost totally silent. The manualists cite only four places where the Church says anything on parvity of matter, none of which deals directly with the question. The most quoted reference by the manualists is to Alexander VII's condemnation of proposition 40 in 1666. The main thrust of the condemnation was to deny the erroneous statement of the laxists on parvity of matter. This condemnation is at best only an implicit argument in favor of the traditional teaching. Secondly, Genicot states that theologians are in doubt as to the real meaning of the proposition. There seems to be some ambiguity in the wording of the proposition itself. Davis point out three other references to the teaching of the Church's magisterium -- a response of the

Holy Office in 1661 concerning solicitation and to statements of Pope Clement VIII and Paul V.

None of the manualists cites Sacred Scripture as a source in defense of their position on parvity of matter. Obviously, Sacred Scripture would not be concerned with such specifics. However, they do quote from St. Paul to support their position concerning the gravity of the complete act.

Only one other external criterion is used by the manualists to bolster their position. Noldin and Davis state that all theologians hold the doctrine of no parvity of matter in sins against the sixth and ninth commandments.

In conclusion, certain facts are most evident from the study of the historical development of the parvity of matter question prior to Vatican II. First, the magisterium of the Church had not spoken definitively on the matter. To look to the Church for support would be fruitless. There is no conclusive magisterial statement in favor of the traditional teaching. Secondly, there seems to be unanimous agreement among theologians in regard to no parvity of matter; they echo each other. Thirdly, the validity of the no parvity of matter teaching is only as strong as the arguments from reason.

1 Edward Genicot, op. cit., pp. 350-354.

2 Ibid., p. 340.

3 Ibid., pp. 347-348.

4 Ibid., p. 348.

5 Ibid.

6 Ibid.

7 H. Noldin, S.J. and A. Schmitt, S.J., <u>Summa Theologiae Moralis</u>: <u>De Sexto Praecepto et De Usu Matrimonii</u>, (Innsbruck: F. Rauch, 1934), P. 11.

8 Ibid., pp. 11-12.

9 Ibid., p. 12.

10 Ibid., p. 13.

11 Ibid.

12 Ibid.

13 Henry Davis, S.J., <u>Moral and Pastoral Theology</u>, Vol. 2, (London: Sheed and Ward, 1935), pp. 180-181.

14 Ibid., p. 181.

15 Ibid., pp. 181-182.

16 H. Denziger and A. Schonmetzer, <u>Enchiridion Symbolorum</u>, n. 2013.

17 Henry Davis, S.J., <u>Moral and Pastoral Theology</u>, p. 182.

18 Ibid.

19 Ibid., pp. 182-183.

20 Ibid., p. 183.

21 J. Aertnys, C.SS.R. and C. A. Damen, C.SS.R., <u>Theologiae Moralis</u>, Tome 1 (Turin: Marietti, 1939), pp. 433-434.

22 Ibid., p. 434.

23 Ibid.

24 Ibid., p. 451.

25 Ibid.

26 Ibid., pp. 451-452.

27 Benedict H. Merkelbach, O.P., *Summa Theologiae Moralis*, 5th edition, Vol. II (Paris: Desclee De Brouwer et Soc., 1946), pp. 934-935.

28 Ibid., p. 935.

29 Ibid.

30 St. Thomas Aquinas, *Summa Theologica*, I-II, 1.

31 Merkelbach, Ibid., p. 936.

32 Ibid., pp. 936-937.

33 Ibid., p. 937.

Chapter III

A Re-Evaluation of Moral Theology
in the Theological Climate Subsequent
to Vatican II

In 1978, Charles Curran wrote in his book, <u>Issues in Sexual and Medical Ethics</u>, that there could be parvity of matter in acts against the sixth and ninth commandments. Obviously, his stance is a radical departure from the traditional teaching in this matter. He states further that many theologians today rightly reject the traditional teaching on parvity of matter.[1]

A three-hundred year old theological teaching is not changed just overnight. New theological insights and teaching need time to expand and to develop. They also need the proper setting in which to form and take shape. Because of the entrenched traditional teaching on parvity of matter, this is especially true of a newly proposed understanding that is taking shape. Not only are theological arguments necessary to justify the teaching, but there has to be also a theological climate, or better a theological ambiance in which new ideas and thoughts can germinate and develop.

In this chapter we will investigate the theological reasons and look at the theological climate which prompted certain theologians to depart from the traditional teaching on parvity of matter and to articulate a new understanding.

The theological climate which occasioned a different approach to parvity of matter can be listed under four headings: the dissatisfaction with the traditional approach to moral theology; the mandate of Vatican II to update and renew all theological disciplines through a more lively attitude to the mystery of Christ and the Bible; a rejection of the manualists' understanding of natural law; and the theory of the fundamental option. All of these provided the climate and had a direct influence on the formulation of a contemporary view on parvity of matter.

The Method of Traditional Moral Theology

According to recent authors reality can be viewed from two perspectives: the classicist world view and the historically conscious world view. These are important factors in studying the methodology of moral theology because it is from one's world view that one develops his or her method.

The classicist world view, since it has its roots in Greek tradition, emphasizes the immutable, the eternal, the static. Growth and progress have little place in this view. Essences and substances are the operative words. Time and history are "accidents" which have little or no effect on the constitution of reality. Essences and substances are immutable, touched only by "accidental" changes.

The historical world view has a dynamic perspective of nature. The world is not static, immutable, but it is, rather, evolving. Progress, growth, and change are the operative words. The cold, sterile, objective order and harmony are not characteristic notes of this world view. Blurring motion and subjective feeling are its characteristic features.[2]

The traditional approach to moral theology was the classical world view approach. Those who advocated this approach believed that the norm for sexual right or wrong could be known through the physical/biological nature. Human nature is conceived as static and unchanging. It is seen as a norm which traverses time and culture. Culture and actions of any age may be judged according to that unchanging nature. Moral absolutes of a very specific nature can very easily be derived from such a firm unchanging base.

This classical world view approach had the advantage, pastorally speaking, of giving a person, faced with a moral decision, a high degree of certainty of the rightness or wrongness of an act. There is a certain clarity that is part and parcel of this approach even when the conclusions do not agree with a person's wants or desires.[3]

However, according to many contemporary moral theologians this classical world view to moral theology had many shortcomings. Robert Springer, S.J. writes that this approach developed a code of morality that was too rigid. "Rules evolved which allowed no exceptions, instead of a flexible set of moral rules going beyond the basic principles." Theoretically, this code of morality admitted the possibility of exception as St. Thomas taught, but in practice in the pulpit and in the classroom this was not the case. The rules were predetermined and predetermining norms of behavior. Springer states that the traditional code of morality, which developed from the classical world view approach, should have been only a guideline for decision-making. This would allow for the specificity (or the <u>contingens singulare</u> of St. Thomas) of each moral choice and the changing situation of mankind. What had developed is rather a computerized morality. Conscience had only to find the right slot or apply the right rule and the answer was almost automatic.[4]

According to Springer this absolutizing tendency of the traditional approach to moral theology led to a distorted type of casuistry. The ready-made, unvarying norms extended beyond the rules of conduct to the level of moral conclusions, to concrete decision-making. The fault was not with casuistry itself, but rather with the way it was taught. Cases were studied in the various areas of moral and solutions were worked out. These cases and their solutions were meant to be only examples, models of what to do in matters of justice, integrity, or chastity. However, this was not the case in practice. The cases became the norm. Moral theologizing became nothing more than connecting a moral judgment with a similar case already worked out in theory to find out what one should do in a given situation.[5]

By the nineteenth century many theologians had grown tired of the negative attitude of moral theology, the legalistic approach, and the casuistry of the manualists. A reaction set in. John Michael Sailer (1751-1832) and John Baptist Hirscher (1788-1865) were the first theologians to attempt a renewal. The thoughts of these two pioneers were carried on and developed by the theologians of the Tubingen school in Germany. The attempts at renewal did not catch on quickly. The work of the Tubingen school was limited within the confines of Germany. The twentieth century brought further attempts at renewal both inside and outside Germany. However, it was not until the time of Bernard Haring that Catholic thinking took the question of renewal in moral theology seriously.[6]

This general feeling of dissatisfaction with the decadent state of moral theology became more visible in the writing of Catholic theologians especially following World War II according to George M. Regan. By the middle of the fifties this same reaction was experienced in the United States and continues to the present day. Regan classifies contemporary criticism of traditional moral theology under two headings. In his view moral theology has become preponderantly a system of philosophical ethics and has little contact with the central mysteries of the Christian faith. His second criticism concerns the method of traditional moral theology. He believes that the modern person has adopted a more historically conscious and evolving world view in place of the traditional classical world view which pervades Catholic moral theology.[7]

In his first criticism of traditional moral theology Regan contends that the discipline isolated itself. The basic points of revelation which were relegated to dogmatic theology became effectively separated. Christ's role and the sanctifying mission of the Holy Spirit received little stress. Moral theology took little note of the sacraments. Baptism and its ensuing commitment to a life of Christian virtue did not serve as the basic starting point. Scripture was employed only to provide supporting arguments for conclusions already reached by reason.

Because moral theology was separated from its Christian sources, it developed its own course and emerged in an unhealthy state. An excessive use of casuistry and a seeming endorsement of minimalism resulted. A negative tone developed because of an excessive stress on sin, on the difference between mortal and venial sins, and on the distinction between precepts and counsels. Positive values faded in the background for the most part and a "thou shalt not" mind-set had the upper hand in forming consciences. Law became the all-important factor in one's life. Living within the law replaced the open-ended morality of love which Jesus preached.[8]

Regan's second criticism against traditional moral theology concerns its method. He writes that the classicist world view of traditional moral theology has been replaced by a newer, a more relevant approach -- the historically conscious world view. This classicist approach sought to determine first principles of morality from which other norms of conduct could be deduced. Since this classicist method was employed by the manualists and their predecessors, one should not be surprised to find in moral theology a stress and emphasis on objective and unchanging standards. Any query could be answered by fitting it into predetermined and neat categories. All a moral theologian had to do was to find the right slot for the right peg. Such a method, according to Regan, reduces the dynamic and inspirational message announced by Jesus to an abstract, static, and torpid condition. Progressive and developing religious thought does not appear.[9]

Many contemporary moral theologians react against this classicist world view. They see the world as constantly evolving. Progress, development, and growth have always been a part of man's history. The historical world view stresses movement and the subjective. The concrete, a posteriori, and inductive reasoning characterize its theological method. The real world is met through the concrete, individual person and thing. The abstract, the absolute, and certitude yield to the concrete, the relative, and doubt. The empirical sciences of psychology, sociology, and anthropology provide important contributions in the historical world view because of the prominence of accidental circumstances.

Regan concludes that because of this clash between world views one can see why many contemporary moral theologians feel the need for renewal. Traditional moral theology fails to answer their needs. Its basic world view, content, and language are not realistic.[10]

Charles Curran strongly endorses this opinion. The crisis in moral theology today is due precisely to the irrelevancy of the traditional mthod. Traditional moral theology is out of touch with real meaning of reality. Since present day moral theology manuals reflect the classicist approach to reality, the new historical world view and a new more-historically conscious methodology will have important consequences when applied to existing moral teachings.[11]

One can see how this general lack of enthusiasm for the traditional way of theologizing produced the climate for renewal in moral theology. By 1960, the stage was set. The need to update and reform moral theology was evident. What was needed for Catholic theologians was official recognition. This came in the form of the Vatican II mandate.

The Mandate of Vatican II

If John XXIII had not convened the Second Vatican Council, the renewal in moral theology among Catholic theologians would have continued to proceed at a very slow pace. The traditional world view and the teaching of the manualists would continue to reign supreme in the field of moral theology. Vatican II was the proximate reason for the renewal of moral theology among Catholic theologians. The fathers of the Council mandated that the traditional teachings of moral theology be brought into contact with reality. Theological disciplines were to be renewed by a livelier and closer contact with the mystery of Christ and Sacred Scripture. The Council fathers singled out moral theology. They mandated that special attention be given to the development of moral theology. "Its (moral theology) scientific exposition should be more thoroughly nourished by scriptural teaching. It should show the nobility of the Christian vocation of the faithful, and their obligation to bring forth fruit in charity for the life of the world should be made manifest and developed."[12]

Joseph Fuchs, S.J. analyzes the reasons for the Council's mandate. Certainly it is not because of moral theology's preeminence over the other theological disciplines. The Council stresses the importance of dogmatic theology for moral theology and points out that many of the problems which human beings experience find their solutions in the light of the revealed eternal truths, expounded in dogmatic theology. The Council fathers state further that Sacred Scripture is the very "soul of all theology" and insist that all theological students get a thorough grounding in the study of Scripture.[13]

Fuchs believes, therefore, that the admonition of the Council fathers to pay attention to moral theology is due to other reasons. There can be no doubt as to the close relationship of moral theology to dogmatic theology and other theological disciplines. But Fuchs states that this relationship is not sufficient reason for the Council fathers to single out moral theology. He says that there is a more compelling reason for the Council's injunction, namely that the traditional presentation of this discipline has left much to be desired.[14]

The Council fathers wanted a positive approach to moral. The renewal in moral and all the other theological disciplines should be effected through a more lively attitude to the mystery of Christ and the history of salvation. Teachers of theology should instill in their students a desire to penetrate these mysteries more deeply and reach a deeper understanding of them through the study of Sacred Scripture and meditation. These mysteries must be recognized as living. They are an active force in the life and liturgy of the Church and are a real source for the solution of many problems affecting people today. Moral theology must draw its content from divine revelation and expound it in the light of faith under the guidance of the magisterium of the Church. Fuchs does not believe that the Council fathers wanted moral theology to be merely a system of abstractions. It must be a discipline that fosters the spiritual growth of its students and furnishes the foundation for the pastoral work of the priesthood.[15]

Fuchs concludes his thoughts on moral theology and Vatican II by saying that the Council fathers clearly define moral theology's goal lest there be any misunderstanding. The fathers of the Council mandated that the content of moral theology with the Bible as its main source should shed light upon "the nobility of the Christian vocation of the faithful and their obligation to bring forth fruit in charity for the life of the world."[16]

Charles Curran also considers Vatican II as the instrumental force in the renewal of moral theology. The documents do not officially endorse any historical world view or classicist method. However, in practice Vatican II definitely portrays a more historically conscious method. The fact that the Council fathers wanted a pastoral orientation is indicative of this method. This pastoral leaning indicates a concern for the Christian faith not as a learning process but as a life to be lived.[17]

Curran believes that the historical world view is reflected in the writings of the Council. The Council fathers admitted that history and human development greatly profited the Church throughout the ages. History reveals much about man and opens new roads to truth. The Church portrayed in Vatican II is a pilgrim Church which grows in truth. Thus, the historical view is very evident in the writings of the Council. In Curran's opinion, even a historically conscious method is used.[18]

In view of the theological direction taken by conciliar statements, two areas of traditional teaching have been receiving special consideration, namely the natural law and one's basic orientation to God.

The Natural Law

One of the basic teachings of the manualists that came under close scrutiny as a result of the Vatican's mandate on renewal was the traditional understanding of the natural law. For the manualists human nature, adequately considered in its relation to self, neighbor, and God, was the objective foundation of the natural moral law. By analyzing this nature and its essential relations one could arrive at a knowledge of general principles and of definite concrete, absolute norms, which could, then, be applied to specific concrete situations.

Many contemporary moral theologians reject this manualist notion of the natural law. They feel that in their judgment it is too rationalistic and deductive in character. The immutability note does not allow this concept of the natural law to keep pace or meet the challenges of other sciences such as put forth in philosophy, theology, sociology, psychology, and cultural anthropology.[19]

Over the period of years since St. Thomas Aquinas, the manualist neo-scholastic notion of the natural law developed a methodology of "physicalism". The biological structure of an act became normative of right and wrong, because in each act there is a God-given finality and structure which human beings must respect.[20]

Many post-Vatican II scholars took issue with the physicalist methodology of the manualists. Charles Curran is highly critical of the method. In his opinion there is no moral value or meaning attached to the biological structure of an act. He cites the Church's teachings on rhythm as an argument in favor of his position. The rhythm method allows one to engage in marital relations, yet with the positive intention of not procreating. Thus, the finality of the conjugal act, procreation, can be intentionally excluded from the act, while at the same time one does not interfere with the act itself. Human experience and practice indicate that contraceptive marital relations can be acts of love. Hence he concluded that for the most part there is no moral value or meaning expressed in the biological structure of the act.[21] However, he does retract a little. Curran states that in a few instances the moral value and the physical structure cannot be separated. He cites by way of example the inseparability of one's personality from one's physical life.[22]

With most contemporary moral theologians and philosophers in opposition to the physicalist approach to moral theology, many other theories to determine the morality of an act have been proposed.

One theory suggests that the reality of being consists not in terms of its principle of operation, but rather in the relationship with others, and ultimately with Being itself. This would mean, therefore, that all moral requirements are grounded in Being, which grounding makes moral value remain objective. All other things and actions are relativized by their relationship to Being. Absolute norms of morality based on the structure of an individual act, viewed in itself apart from the relationship with other beings and the fullness of being, have no validity. Morality depends not only on determinate facts of a situation, but also on the concrete possibilities which man's presence to Being opens up to him. In this theory the ultimate norm of morality is the law of intelligent responsiveness or, in other terms, the law of discerning love. Morally good acts embody such responsiveness, morally bad acts are in opposition to it. A moral person lives for Being and seeks to promote its reign in every situation. Being moral is being reasonable to the fullest sense, if one takes reason as the faculty of the Absolute which opens us to Being and enables us to conduct our actions accordingly.[23]

A second theory judges the morality of an action on whether or not the action builds up or tears down the community. This building up or tearing down always happens in a determined way, completely dependent on the concrete requirements of a community. There are some visible external constants always present, but there are also subforms that are always changing. For example, what was considered a mutilation in one era can be considered a transplantation in a later era. Changes in the community -- a mere enlightened medical science -- makes this possible. Killing, for example, can sometimes be a service to a community, if the community recognizes it as such. A community can execute a murderer and even the one who kills the murderer on his own initiative. The welfare of the community is the norm of morality.[24]

A third theory views morality in relationship to the good of man. It proposes that the real basis of the natural moral law is the welfare of mankind. Man's good is the criterion and goal of love and of all natural law. Christ did not offer any ready-made solutions to existing or future moral problems which man would face throughout the centuries. He provided the basis for all solutions by proclaiming the love of God and neighbor as the supreme all-embracing law. All existing moral laws look to the good of man and man solves all new moral problems on the basis of what is good for the welfare of mankind. Even though the formulation of moral judgments which are imposed on man are developed locally and regionally by cultural or religious society, nevertheless the determination of all general moral law is not the task of one cultural group or religious body -- not even the Catholic Church, but of the whole of mankind and especially of the more prudent and responsible members.[25]

Some theologians feel that all the evidence is not yet in for determining a norm of morality. As still a fourth possible theory, John Milhaven suggests that there exists in contemporary theology two approaches to moral evaluation. Both approaches base their moral judgment on the "purpose" of a prospective action, but differ in their understanding of morally decisive purpose. The traditional approach looks to the specific purpose of an action and maintains that the ultimate purpose and the good of man will be attained. On the other hand, the contemporary approach measures the action directly in the light of man's general purpose: a life of understanding and love. In this approach the general purpose coincides with the specific end. However, the problem presents itself in assessing the proportionate value of an action which has many purposes. Milhaven responds that neither mere regularity nor degree of convergence reveal this proportionate value. It is rather the evidence of the probable or certain consequences of the action, which defines the hierarchy of purposes. In other words, what is going to result from the act in question? The acquisition of this evidence requires observation, correlation, and the weighing out of numerous facts. According to Milhaven, it is this process that reveals the value of most human acts. It points up the effects that these acts will have in the concrete, existing world on those absolute values which one discerns by immediate insight.[26]

Even though contemporary moral theologians differ in their formulation of a norm of morality, still there is almost unanimous agreement among them in their dissent concerning an even more basic question -- the manualists' understanding of the existence of objective moral evil. For years the manualists and their predecessors taught that some actions apart from their ends and circumstances were morally evil. Such acts as the violation of the marriage contract, the direct taking of an innocent life, and the free exercise of one's sexual faculty outside of marriage were the cited examples of objectively morally evil actions. These acts were classified by the manualists as evil <u>ex</u> <u>toto</u> <u>genere</u> <u>suo</u>, or intrinsically evil, or objectively grave. Such acts are absolute in nature. They admit of no exception under any circumstances.[27]

Many modern day theologians feel that the objective morality of an action should be determined from the concrete totality of the action. Unlike the manualists, they hold that every human act in itself contains evil. However, this evil is not the same as moral evil. Contemporary moral theologians call this evil as opposed to moral evil by a variety of names. Louis Janssens calls this evil ontic evil.[28] Josef Fuchs calls it premoral evil.[29] Bruno Schuller[30] and Richard McCormick[31] use the term nonmoral evil. Whatever name by which this evil is called, it is used to express the lack of perfection in everything human. Ontic or premoral evil expresses human limitation in an act. It expresses the failure of man to reach complete human actualization. Such acts as suffering, injury, fatigue, ignorance, violence, and death, which the manualists termed physical evils, are examples of ontic evil. Even though these acts are part and parcel of the human situation, they are evil because they are detrimental to full human growth. Louis Janssens writes that ontic evil is part of our every action because we are in time and space, live together in the same material world, and are involved and act in a common situation. Thus, moral good and ontic evil can co-exist in the same act. We cannot do a moral good without causing or admitting to some ontic evil. According to Janssens, moral evil is causing or permitting ontic evil without a proportionate reason. It is never in the act itself.[32]

The act in itself is pre-moral or nonmoral. The objective moral rightness or wrongness of an act stems partly from the end and the circumstances of an action to such a degree that morality is never determined from the act by itself. It is more consistent with the teachings of St. Thomas Aquinas to see the object, the end, and the circumstances as a part of a continuum so that moral evil never comes from any one of them, apart from the other two. The ramification of this teaching for the parvity of matter doctrine in sexual sins is obvious. An act, for example, which produces venereal pleasure could be performed and not considered serious matter if the purpose of the act is good and if a proportionate reason for allowing the premoral evil (the act) exists.[33]

The Fundamental Option

As a result of the Vatican mandate to re-evalute and update traditional teachings in moral theology, the traditional notion and doctrine of sin came under consideration. The case of falling in and out of God's favor through serious sin was studied in light of biblical research and the findings of religious anthropology.[34]

Most of the pre-Vatican II textbooks on moral theology defined sin as the breaking of God's law. Contemporary moral theologians do not question the need of laws and rules; they question, rather, whether or not lawbreaking should be considered the essential element in the definition of sin. They see law as measuring what is on the surface of the person, whereas sin seems to come from a deeper level. In developing their notion of sin, contemporary theologians feel that they find such evidence in Scripture.

The biblical notion of sin is closely related to the idea of covenant. Sin is a violation and a rupture of covenant with the living God. Sin is committed, in New Testament understanding, when one excludes the new covenant bond from one's life. Through sin one ruptures the new covenant in one's whole personality. Christ no longer exists for the sinner. In sinning, one says, "no" to God, but in a much more definitive way than the manualists ever taught or even understood. Contemporary moralists cite such New Testament passages as Luke 15, 1 John, Galatians 2:20, and Romans 7:20 in support of this covenant notion of sin.[35]

In Luke 15, the Parable of the Prodigal Son, the evangelist contrasts the pharisaical act-concept of sin with the covenant concept. The elder brother's allegiance to his father is merely act-oriented. There is no depth to that life. As long as he toed the line, as long as he was not disobedient or disloyal, or dissolute in his living, he considered himself a good son, even though devoid of real feeling for this father. There was no underlying substance to his acts. He was just going through the motions. Avoidance of sin for him meant solely external observance. Thus, St. Luke portrays through the action of the elder son that external acts are not necessarily indicative of inner disposition.

In the person of the Prodigal Son, on the other hand, the evangelist points out the real meaning of sin. He contrasts external acts and inner disposition. The Prodigal does not lament a series of evil external acts. He is more concerned with the broken commitment, the severed bond between himself and his father. The external acts -- the desertion, the squandering of the inheritance, the dissolute living -- are not viewed by St. Luke as convenant-breaking, but rather as symptoms or manifestations of a fundamental malaise, which is actually the breaking of the sonship convenant between the Prodigal and his father. The father's joy is not the result of the son's safe return. It is the result of the restoration of the sonship convenant. Real sin, according to St. Luke, therefore, consists not in external actions, but in an evil disposition.[36]

In 1 John, the same covenant notion of sin is found. John writes, "He who is born of God cannot sin" (3:9) and "He who commits sin is of the Evil one" (3:10). As long as one commits oneself to God, as long as one lives in the filial relationship to God, then one cannot sin. The constant awareness of this covenant in one's heart is the secret of a sinless life. However, if one does sin, the covenant is broken and a new one springs into being, a new relationship with the devil. Thus St. John feels that the real significance of sin is not basically the fact of an evil act in which one defies God. It is more the establishment of a total personality -- involving relationship with a new God, the Evil one.[37]

The fact of covenant and broken covenant is also considered in the writing of St. Paul. He describes the covenant with God when he writes to the Galatians, "I live, now not I, but it is Christ that lives in me" (2:20). This covenant is not unbreakable. It can be supplanted with another covenant, a covenant with the Evil One. Paul acknowledges this when he tells the Romans, "If I sin, it is not so much I that sin, as the power of sin that dwells in me" (7:20). In these passages Paul is considering sin not so much as a series of external acts. He considers sin as an evil disposition, a pact or covenant with the devil.[38]

With this biblical notion of sin as a background, post-Vatican II theologians sought to reformulate the manualists' act-oriented concept of sin in accordance with the biblical notion of covenant.[39] John Glaser writes that the idea of a fully vibrant commitment to God one moment, snuffed out through sin in another, and being restored to its original state in a third does not seem to have validity in reality. Contemporary psychologists argue that in our relationship of friendship with other human beings there is an element of stability. Friendships have the ability to sustain multiple hurts before being broken. Some theologians, therefore, argue that our relationship with God should have the same resiliency.[40]

Post-Vatican II theologians have rethought this area of Christian responsiblity. Contrary to the traditional stance, they feel that man's deep-rooted commitment to God is not destroyed by every serious sin. As in other human relationships, they feel that there is greater stability in this relationship than was previously taught. The development of this contemporary theme of Christian responsibility has a direct effect on the traditional understanding of sin and the traditional teaching on parvity of matter in the sixth and ninth commandments.[41]

In discussing this contemporary theme of Christian responsibility, John Glaser writes that man's freedom can no longer be viewed on a unidimensional level. Psychology shows us that it is multidimensional in nature. No longer does one free act necessarily reflect man's basic commitment to God. Rather, man is structured in a series of concentric circles on various strata. Man's core freedom is found in the center of these concentric circles on the deepest level. It is only on this deepest level that man loves, acts, chooses in the fullest sense of these terms. It is only on this level, therefore, that man commits himself as a lover or sinner.[42]

Everyone sometime or other in his life assumes in the very core of his person a basic choice for or against God. Not all one's subsequent acts share in this fundamental freedom. In terms of a multidimensional man, one can speak of man's basic choice, which refers to his use of fundamental freedom in contrast to various peripheral choices, which involve only a lesser degree of freedom. It is only in this basic choice that man disposes himself before God and the world in an ultimate, total, and definitive way. His specific or peripheral choices, which concern daily mundane matters, may either manifest or veil his basic choice.[43]

Bruno Schuller, S.J. states that an individual can affirm one moral value and at the same time reject another, even though the latter is intrinsically connected with the former. According to his thinking, an individual can, on the one hand, definitely decide to do God's will, and yet willingly do that which is contrary to His will without negating his previous decision. Such an act would destroy the inner unity of the individual if both occurred in the same way. This, however, is not the case. The unity of the person is preserved because the decision to do God's will is affirmed from the center, the very core of the person, whereas he rejects that will from a more peripheral dimension of his person.[44]

As an illustration of Schuller's thoughts, contemporary theologians present the case of a woman, who is both wife and mother, imprisoned in a concentration camp. In this case this woman knows that she can secure release from prison to join her husband and her family if she becomes a burden to prison officials because of illness or pregnancy. Realizing the one value that adultery is prohibited by Almighty God and wanting to follow His will, nevertheless, without negating her desire to follow God's law, she freely becomes pregnant by a prison guard in order to secure her release. According to Schuller, the unity of the woman can be preserved if one posits the two dimensions of a person's freedom.[45]

A similar case is related by St. Augustine in his Commentary on the Lord's Sermon on the Mount. It seemed that a certain man owed the public treasury a pound of gold. Since he was unable to provide the sum, he offers to allow his wife to indulge the carnal desires of another man through carnal intercourse to secure the pound of gold. Because the wife's motive for submitting was devoid of any lustful desire and was based exclusively on her great love for him, Augustine concluded that the woman's action might have been justified and was not necessarily adulterous.46 Modern day theologians would say that her act proceeded from her peripheral freedom. Because of the shallow nature of this peripheral freedom, acts which flow from that level will not have the same degree of stability as those which flow from the very center of the person. Thus, the external conduct arising from such a peripheral level will be more apt to fluctuate between affirmation and rejection.47

As one might suspect, the new theory in Christian responsibility has caused a change in the traditional sin classification. Some contemporary theologians see a threefold division as opposed to the traditional venial and mortal categories. Mortal sinfulness is that state which implies a change of one's basic option. The same objective moral action might be a mortal sin for one person, but not for another. For example, the decision to omit Sunday Mass might well be the final step for the external expression of a state of mind that has already rejected or become alienated from God. The same act for a second person could be nothing more than laziness or a bout of depression, leaving intact one's basic orientation toward God. Some contemporary moral theologians add a category of sin which would stand between the traditional mortal/venial sin categories. Serious or grave sins, which in the tradition are classified as mortal, do not break the fundamental commitment. They do not imply a total alienation from God.48

The questioning of the traditional categories of sin is not a recent development in contemporary moral theology. It pre-dates the Second Vatican Council. As early as 1947, Joanne Manya wrote about three type of sin as opposed to the traditional mortal/venial sin categories. Manya accepts the traditional understanding of venial sin. Like the manualists he sees it as a disorder, but not an abandonment of Almighty God. One who sins only venially always retains his relationship to his final end. Manya cites St. Thomas Aquinas in support of the notion that sin is not necessarily a total breaking with Almighty God. In his <u>Summa Contra Gentiles</u>, Thomas states that even when man sins he retains the capability of repentance. This desire of man to repent and his guilt after having committed a sin are signs that one has this capability. One actually removes the disorder when the grace of repentance operates in his soul.49 Thus, according to St. Thomas, even in the presence of the disorder of sin, one can retain his love for God.50

Manya also accepts the traditional understanding of mortal sin. It is seen as the turning away from Almighty God and a turning toward a creature. In essence, it is the substituting of the creature in the place of God. It is making the creature one's final end. Because mortal sin deals with one's final end, the manualists see the turning from God as complete and definitive.51

Taking the two elements of mortal sins -- the turning from God and the turning towards a creature -- Manya posits a third type of sin. He feels that many mortal sins which are committed by men are not the total rejection of Almighty God, but are similar in nature to venial sins. In his opinion, these types of sins are distinct from the strict mortal sin and venial sin of the manualists. They seem to hold a middle place between them. Sins in this third category do not have the total and explicit rejection of God, but only an implicit and partial rejection. The adherence to God as one's final end remains constant. The possibility of restoring total friendship with Almighty God is possible by simply restoring the proper order in one's life. One has to remove whatever is preventing loving God above all things. According to Manya, in this third category of sin, the sinner turns toward creatures and, in this sense, the act is similar to the traditional understanding of mortal sin, even though there is no explicit rejection of God. On the other hand, since this explicit rejection is lacking, sins in this third category are similar to the traditional understanding of venial sin. Thus, Manya has laid the foundation for the threefold classification of sin by those who espouse the fundamental option theory -- mortal sin, serious sin, and venial sin.52

Kevin F. O'Shea, C.SS.R. writes that in this serious sin category there is certainly the element of mortal sin. There is a weakening of the covenant, there is the selfish realization of the person against God. However, serious sin differs from mortal sin in that the consequent sin-dynamism is absent and the personality of the sinner is not affected as sinful unto death. O'Shea says that in such a case, the climate, the atmosphere, the spiritual air in which the person is immersed, Christ's presence and love, prevent the reversal of one's basic choice. The self-position against God and the weakening of one's covenant with God are certainly present in such sins. However, one's inner commitment to God remains. One's covenant life is envisaged and even expected to continue in the future.53

The third category of sins which theologians identify is the traditional venial grouping. Sins of this type are the ordinary minor failings of daily life. They are sins of weakness, the delays, halts, and minor detours of the person sincerely trying to walk in the path of goodness.54

Charles Curran summarizes the distinction between mortal and venial sin in the same way. According to his interpretation, the difference between serious and light sin lies in the existential involvement of the subject in a particular action. Mortal sin is one which involves a fundamental option, whereas venial sins remains a more superficial and peripheral action, not involving the core of the person.

Curran applies the same distinction to grave and light matter. Grave matter is that which will ordinarily engage the depth of one's person in the action. Light matter, on the other hand, will not ordinarily involve the core of one's personality in the action. Such matter indicates that the action will for the most part be superficial and peripheral, and not a fundamental choice. Many of our daily actions have this peripheral aspect and do not involve our persons.[55]

Summary

Any changes in the method of a physical science of its fundamental principles have repercussions on the established teachings of that science. This is also true in the discipline of theology. The theological changes, developed in this chapter, have a great effect on many of the traditional teaching in moral theology, since they involve a change in method and fundamental principles. These changes permit contemporary moral theologians to break with many of the entrenched teachings of the manualists, but more specifically they set the stage for the affirmation of parvity of matter in sins against the sixth and ninth commandments.

The general dissatisfaction with the manualists' classicist approach to moral theology certainly provided the occasion for rethinking and updating many of the traditional theological teachings since 1900. Notwithstanding the fact that this actual updating process in moral would have taken place at a much earlier date had it not been for the extreme centralization of Catholicism around the papacy, nevertheless it would not have occurred when it did, if the Vatican II mandate had not appeared on the scene. In the documents the fathers of the Council encouraged and even commissioned Catholic theologians to rethink and to update the traditional teachings of theology, especially moral theology.

The manualists lost their main argument in favor of no parvity of matter in the reshaping of the traditional understanding of the natural law. They identified the natural law with a physicalist approach to morality. Thus, for the manualists, the main argument in favor of the traditional teaching on parvity of matter was rooted in the finality of the generative act. The act itself and any degree of actuation, no matter how slight, and its accompanying venereal pleasure, which is serious matter, are ordered towards that end. With the rejection of this physicalist approach to morality by contemporary theologians, the manualists' argument for no parvity of matter loses its validity and the consequent malice of desiring venereal pleasure apart from a procreation orientation disappears.

Even though modern-day theologians reject the physicalist approach to moral law, and, thereby, undermine the manualists' teaching on parvity of matter, still the question remains whether or not one can in certain circumstances deliberately seek venereal pleasure without destroying the love relationship between the individual and his creator. The fundamental option theory allows for parvity of matter in sins against the sixth and ninth commandments. Those who espouse this theory question whether every venereal thought or action necessarily implies a rupture of the basic commitment which one has with Almighty God. These theologians believe that some of those acts, though serious matter and deliberately sought, could possibly originate in the peripheral freedom sphere, which would classify them as serious sins but not mortal, thereby opening the door for parvity of matter in sins against the sixth and ninth commandments.

1 "I deny there is no parvity of matter in sexuality. At the very most, the concept of grave matter constitutes a presumptive judgment that such matter is of so great importance that it will ordinarily involve a fundamental option and break the relationship of love ... Today many theologians rightly reject such a teaching." Charles E. Curran, Issues in Sexual and Medical Ethics (Notre Dame: University of Notre Dame Press, 1978), pp. 45-46.

2 Bernard Lonergan, S.J., "The Transition from a Classicist World View to Historical Mindedness" Law for Liberty, ed. J. Biechler (Baltimore: Helicon Press, 1967), pp. 126-133.

3 Rev. Robert M. Friday, "Adults Making Responsible Moral Decisions," National Conference of Diocesan Directors of Religious Education Resource Paper, 1979, p. 113.

4 "Concretely, the fixation was evidenced in that it had become a code of morality. Instead of a flexible set of moral rules going beyond the basic principles in the area of moral, these rules were elevated to the status of universal unexceptionable principle." Robert H. Springer, S.J., "Conscience, Behavioral Science and Absolutes" in Absolutes in Moral Theology?, ed. Charles Curran, (Washington, D.C.: Corpus Instrumentorum, Inc., 1968), p. 20.

5 Ibid., pp. 20-21.

6 Charles E. Curran, A New Look at Christian Morality (Notre Dame: Fides Publishers, Inc., 1968), pp. 146-147. For an understanding of Bernard Haring's great contributions to moral theology, one may consult his following works: The Law of Christ, trans. Edwin G. Kaiser (Westminster, ed.: Newman Press, 1961), Toward a Christian Moral Theology (Notre Dame: University of Notre Dame Press, 1966), Morality is for Persons (New York: Farrar, Straus and Giroux, 1971) and Free and Faithful in Christ (New York: The Seabury Press, 1978).

7 George M. Regan, C.M., New Trends in Moral Theology (New York: Newman Press, 1971), pp. 33-34.

8 Ibid., pp. 33-34.

9 Ibid., p. 34.

10 Ibid., pp. 34-35.

11 Charles E. Curran, "Absolute Norms and Medical Ethics" in Absolutes in Moral Theology?, p. 132.

12 Vatican II, "Decree on Priestly Formation", The Documents of Vatican II ed. Walter M. Abbott, S.J. (New York: Corpus Books, 1966), p. 452.

13 Ibid., p. 451.

14 Josef Fuchs, S.J., Human Values and Christian Morality (Dublin: Gill and Macmillan, 1970), pp. 1-2.

15 Ibid., p. 2.

16 Ibid., pp. 2-3; cf. "Optatam Totius", op.cit.

17 Charles E. Curran, "Absolute Norms and Medical Ethics", Absolutes in Moral Theology?, p. 129.

18 Ibid., pp. 129-131.

19 William E. May, "Natural Law," New Catholic Encyclopedia Vol. XVII (Washington, D.C.: Publishers Guild, Inc., 1978), p. 460.

20 Sean Fagan, S.J., Has Sin Changed? (Garden City, New York: Image Books, 1979), pp. 62-63.

21 Charles E. Curran, Transition and Tradition in Moral Theology (Notre Dame: University of Notre Dame Press, 1979), p. 32.

22 Ibid.

23 Robert O. Johann, S.J., "Responsible Parenthood: A Philosophical View," Proceedings of the Catholic Theological Society of America 20 (1965): 115-128.

24 William van der Marck, Love and Fertility (London: Sheed and Ward, 1965), pp. 35-63.

25 Francis Simons, "The Catholic Church and the New Morality" Cross Currents 16 (1966): 429-445.

26 John G. Milhaven, S.J., "Toward an Epistemology of Ethics", Theological Studies, 27 (June 1966): 228-241.

27 Timothy E. O'Connell, Principles for a Catholic Morality (New York: The Seabury Press, 1978), pp. 165-169.

28 Louis Janssens, "Ontic Evil and Moral Evil", in Reading in Moral Theology No. 1, ed. Charles E. Curran and Richard A. McCormick (New York: Paulist Press, 1979), p. 60.

29 Joseph Fuchs, S.J., "The Absoluteness of Moral Terms", in Readings in Moral Theology No. 1., p. 118.

30 Bruno Schuller, S.J., "Direct Killing/Indirect Killing", in Readings in Moral Theology No. 1., p. 144.

31 Richard McCormick, S.J., Ambiguity in Moral Choice, 1973 Pere Marquette Theology Lecture, Marquette University, pp. 53-59.

32 Louis Janssens, "Ontic Evil and Moral Evil", op. cit., pp. 60-61.

33 Philip S. Keane, S.S., Sexual Morality: A Catholic Perspective, (New York: Paulist Press, 1977), pp. 46-49.

34 Cf. Bernard J. F. Lonergan, " Cognitional Structure", Collection: Papers by Bernard Lonergan ed., F. E. Crowe (New York: Herder and Herder, 1967), pp. 221-239; Karl Rahner, "Dogmatic Reflections on the Knowledge and Self-Consciousness of Christ", Theological Investigations, 4, pp. 107-109.

35 Kevin F. O'Shea, C.S.S.R., "The Reality of Sin: A Theological and Pastoral Critique", Theological Studies 29 (June 1968): 241-243.

36 Ibid., p. 243.

37 Ibid., p. 243-244.

38 Ibid., p. 244. CF. R. Koch, Grace et liberte humaine: Reflexion theologique sur Genese I - XI (Paris 1967); S. Lyonnet, "Peche: Dans le judaisme, Dans le nouveau Testament, Peche original," Dictionnaire de la Bible, Supplement 7 (Paris, 1966): 480-567; L. Hartmann, "Sin," Encyclopedic Dictionary of the Bible (New York, 1963) cols. 2218-32; A. Gelin, "Le peche dans l'ancient Testament," Theologie du Peche I, (Paris, 1960); 49-125; Piet Schoonenberg, S.J., Man and Sin (Notre Dame, Inc.: University of Notre Dame Press, 1965), PP. 98-123.

39 Pierre Fransen, S.J., "Toward a Psychology of Divine Grace," Lumen Vitae, XII (1957): 203-243; Bernard Haring, Sin in the Secular Age (Garden City, N.Y.: Doubleday, 1974): T. Hart, "Sin in the Context of the Fundamental Option," Homiletic and Pastoral Review, 71 (1970): 47-50; D. O'Callaghan, "What is Mortal Sin." Furrow, 25 (1974): 71-87: Karl Rahner, S.J., "Reflections on the Unity of Love of Neighbor and the Love of God," Theological Investigations, Vol VI, pp. 231-249.

40 John W. Glaser, S.J., "Transition Between Grace and Sin", Theological Studies 29 (June 1968): 260-261. C.F. also M. Flick, S.J. and Z. Alszeghy, S.J., L'opzione fondamentale della vita morale e la grazia," Gregorianum XLI (1960): 593-619; Bernard Haring, Sin in the Secular Age (Garden City, N.Y.: Doubleday, 1974); Richard A. McCormick, S.J., "The Moral Theology of Vatican II," The Future of Ethics and Theology (Chicago: Argus Communication, 1968), pp. 7-18; Bruno Schuller, S.J., Gesetz und Freiheit (Dusseldorf: Patmos, 1966); J. Fuchs, S.J., Human Values and Christian Morality (Dublin: Gill and Macmillan, 1970); E. McDonagh, "The Moral Subject," Irish Theological Quarterly 39 (1972): 3-22; L. Monden, Sin, Liberty, and Law (New York: Sheed and Ward, 1965); J. Metz, "Freedom as a Threshold Problem between Philosophy and Theology," Philosophy Today 10 (1966): 264-279.

41 Sean Fagan, S.M., op. cit., pp. 86-87.

42 John W. Glaser, S.J., op. cit., pp. 261-262.

43 Josef Fuchs, S.J., op. cit., pp. 94-104.

44 Bruno Schuller, S.J., Gesetz und Freiheit (Dusseldorf: Patmos Verlag, 1966), PP. 101-102.

45 Dennis J. Doherty, "The Tradition in History", in Dimensions of Human Sexuality, ed, Dennis Doherty (Garden City, New York: Doubleday and Company: 1979), p. 60.

46 "I do not argue either side; one can judge whatever they want: the incident has no foundation in divine sources: but as the story is related, our moral sense is not so ready to denounce what that woman did, even with her husband's permission, as we were shocked before when the case was presented to us without any specific example" St. Augustine, De Sermone Domini in Monte, p. 34, 1254.

47 John W. Glaser, S.J., op. cit., p. 165.

48 Sean Fagan, S.M., op. cit., pp. 87-88.

49 St. Thomas Aquinas, Summa Contra Gentiles, II, 156.

50 Joanne B. Manya, Theologumena, Vol. 1: De ratione peccati poenam inducentis (Barcelona: Duran and Bas, 1947), p. 164.

51 Ibid., p. 155.

52 Ibid., pp. 164-165.

53 Kevin F. O'Shea, C.SS.R., op. cit., p. 249.

54 Sean Fagan, S.M., op. cit., p. 88.

55 Charles E. Curran, <u>A New Look at Christian Morality</u>, pp. 206-207.

Chapter IV

Methodological Objections to the Traditional Teaching of No Parvity of Matter

With Vatican II's mandate of freedom given to theologians to rethink and update traditional teachings in theology, it should come as no surprise that the manualists' teaching of no parvity of matter would come under this review. For centuries moral theologians accepted this traditional teaching on the basis of tradition and obedience to the magisterium. After Vatican II because of a new theological climate, which we saw developed in the last chapter, methodological objections to the teaching appeared. Certain theologians began to question the validity of that tradition and to suggest new fundamental principles which would allow for the teaching of parvity of matter in re sexuali.

The methodological objections against the traditional teaching of no parvity of matter are centered in four areas of contemporary theological thought: a rethinking of the traditional understanding of objective morality, a re-evaluation of the traditional teaching of quantitative measurement of objective evil, the fundamental option theory, and a new understanding of human sexuality.

Objective Morality

One area of updating in contemporary moral theology which directly challenges the traditional teaching on parvity of matter is the question of premoral evil and moral evil in the objective order. Josef Fuchs writes that there is a real distinction between the two. Killing, wounding, lying, sterilizing are premoral evils, not necessarily moral evils in themselves. A premoral evil becomes a moral evil when it is taken up as an evil in the intention. This occurs when there is no proportionate reason for causing the premoral evil. According to Fuchs, the moral quality of an act cannot be determined from the action in itself. In this sense his view differs from the traditional understanding of object, circumstance, and intention.[1]

Traditional moralists relied heavily on the goodness or badness found in the act itself. They taught that certain objects were morally evil in themselves and that a good intention could not purify them. The object determined the basic morality of such acts. It also distinguished mortal from venial sin. Since the manualists considered the matter the primary determinant of objective morality, it followed that the act would be the principal determinant of the gravity of the sin. The same holds true for venial sin. If the matter of a particular act is not serious, then the morality of that act would be light. The manualists, therefore, could speak of parvity and gravity of matter in the objective order because in their understanding matter in itself, apart from any circumstances or intention of the agent, can be a moral evil and this evil can admit of degrees in itself.[2]

Fuchs disagrees with this traditional understanding of objective morality. He writes that a moral judgment of an action may not be made in anticipation of the agent's intention since it would not be the judgment of a human act. The object must be considered simultaneously with the intention of the agent and circumstances before the true meaning of the action, its true moral character, can be stated.[3]

Timothy O'Connell agrees with Fuchs except for one slight difference. He qualifies Fuchs's teaching by opting for a single font of morality. Like Fuchs, O'Connell states that one cannot speak of the moral goodness or badness of matter in itself. The traditional teaching of no parvity of matter in re sexuali has no validity. The objective goodness or badness of a particular act is determined by a consideration of the deed itself and the relevant circumstances taken together. According to O'Connell, these two components comprise the font of objective morality.[4]

Those contemporary moral theologians who hold the fundamental option theory of morality also reject the traditional understanding of objective morality. They admit the existence of objective evil, but they feel that the gravity or lack of seriousness of a particular act has nothing to do with the gravity of the sin. A sin is mortal or venial depending upon the degree of personal involvement of the one who performs the act. A mortal sin is one in which a person's core freedom is involved: a venial sin is one in which that depth of freedom is absent. O'Connell sums up this position by stating that either we are part of what we are doing or we are not. If a person's core freedom is not involved in an act, then the gravity of the matter will change nothing. All such a person does is commit a venial sin which in the objective order has serious matter as one of its components.[5]

Philip S. Keane breaks with the manualists' teaching concerning objective morality and, more specifically, on the magisterium's stand on venereal pleasure and parvity of matter. He feels that both concepts should be reformulated. The many debates concerning the morality of venereal pleasure outside of marriage over the years and the many new contemporary approaches to moral theology indicate that such a reformulation is necessary.[6]

In his approach Keane tries to bridge the traditional teaching with contemporary thoughts. He states that all nonmarital venereal pleasure except that pleasure which arises as a result of fleeting thoughts which do not involve the individual in any notable way is evil. However, this evil is not understood in the traditional sense of the word. It is not moral evil that is present, but rather ontic. It is an evil which lacks in a morally significant degree the fulness of being that human beings are capable of achieving through sexual acts. Ontic evil is present not only in the venereal acts of the unmarried, but even the venereal pleasure of the married can contain significant degrees. The exact degree of ontic evil contained in acts causing venereal pleasure can vary with circumstances of age, maturity, and so on.[7]

Keane argues that ontic evil and moral evil are two different types of evil. Some venereal actions in themselves contain ontic evil. This does not necessarily imply that such actions are objectively morally grave. The gravity of the matter of venereal acts is judged by looking at those acts in the totality of the concrete circumstances and the reality in which they occur. If under these conditions a proportionate reason exists to justify the positing of ontically evil venereal pleasure, one may allow the pleasure to occur and even seek it without its being an objectively grave moral evil. On the other hand, if a proportionate reason does not exist to justify the ontic evil, the permitting or positing of venereal pleasure is an objectively grave moral evil. Even in this latter case, however, Keane is quick to point out that such a situation does not necessarily mean mortal sin is present. He does opt for the traditional requirements for mortal sin. The presence or absence of mortal sin depends on the quality of one's consent and the understanding of the objectively grave moral evil.[8]

Keane is unique in his approach in trying to blend traditional theology with newer insights. He feels that his theory is true to the traditional teaching. His use of morally significant ontic evil allows him to stay within the traditional teaching that directly sought venereal pleasure outside marriage is an occasion for serious human reflection and a challenge to human growth and integration.[9] In his view such pleasure is never minor or completely indifferent, as some of his contemporaries teach. Keane also feels that his theory of morality honors the traditional distinction between objective moral evil and mortal sin.[10]

Not only does Keane think that his proposal is in line with the traditional teaching on the morality of venereal pleasure, he even believes that it further develops the teaching. The manualists taught that in reference to venereal pleasure objective evil was moral and was always present to the same degree. In Keane's proposal significant ontic evil is always present, but it can be light matter or serious matter. Secondly, Keane feels that he adds to the traditional teaching by pointing out that the ontic evil contained in venereal pleasure for the unmarried is also present in the venereal pleasure of the married and can be gravely serious, when sex is used in an exploitative and manipulative manner. Keane's third contribution to the tradition is the insistence on the need for discernment in sexual decisions. He admits that it was part of the tradition in the distant past, but in recent times it has not been given its due. Keane's fourth contribution to the development of the traditional teaching consists in distinguishing ontic evil from moral evil. He appeals to the use of proportionate reason for positing the act to determine whether or not ontically evil venereal pleasure is also morally evil. Thus, it would seem that the non-married can directly seek venereal pleasure when the totality of the act contains a proportionate reason for causing or allowing the ontic evil. This ontic evil is not intended by the individual as a moral evil. It is permitted purely as part of a total human action. The overall goodness of this total human action allows this positing of an ontic evil because the fulness of good is never obtainable in this finite and sinful world.[11]

Keane believes that his approach to the whole question of the morality of venereal pleasure maintains a real continuity with the Church's traditional teaching. At the same time he recognizes that this traditional teaching needs to be developed in contemporary moral theology through the application of philosophical insights about morality which were lacking in the past.[12]

The Traditional Categories of Measurement of Objective Evil

The second area of contemporary moral theology which directly questions the traditional teaching of no parvity of matter <u>in re sexuali</u> concerns the categories of measurement of objective evil. The manualists obviously taught that matter apart from circumstances and intention falls into either light or serious categories. In their minds there is such a thing as light and serious matter in itself. The Church has always taught that certain sins were always grave of their very nature. Homicide, adultery, the denial of one's faith have been considered more serious than other acts. Other kinds of acts are not always objectively grave because they do not directly attack persons and their fundamental goods, and because something morally different is done in various degrees. To steal, for example, a small amount of money from a rich person is not related to love precisely in the same way as taking a large sum from a poor man.[13]

Bernard Haring, C.SS.R. opposes all types of quantitative measurement in the area of sin. Prior to Vatican II, he writes, various catechisms had a fixed formula for determining mortal and venial sin. If one transgressed the law of God in a grave matter with full knowledge and freedom, the sin was considered mortal. On the other hand, if the transgression of the law was in a relatively small matter, then the sin was venial. These formulations, according to Haring, imply that an accurate line can be drawn between grave and less serious matter. How such a difference can account for a total qualitative difference between mortal and venial sin is left unanswered. Haring feels that any measurement of matter is depersonalizing and totally unacceptable in contemporary moral theology. Any teaching in which a small degree of disorder would explain the absolutely qualitative difference between hell and purgatory gives a distorted image of God and can be a real temptation against faith.[14]

Haring states that it is impossible to claim common doctrine or an established tradition for the manualists' teaching on parvity of matter. A historical analysis of the development of the doctrine shows that the doctrine took on different meanings and often met with strong opposition from some recognized moral theologians. Haring does admit, however, that the Congregation for the Doctrine of Faith in its recent document on matters concerning sexual morality confirmed the manualists' teaching on parvity of matter as the Church's teaching and Christian tradition.[15] Nevertheless, he contends that modern-day moral theologians want the same norms for the sixth and ninth commandments as for the other commandments. Biblically, it is not feasible to accept smallness of matter with respect to fraternal love, justice, and peace, while asserting in matters of chastity that everything is serious.[16]

In order to acheive this uniformity, Haring takes as his starting point the traditional teaching that every perfectly deliberate and free act against any of God's commandments is, in principle, serious matter and can be a venial sin solely because of a lack of full deliberation or freedom on the part of the agent. He applies this principle to all the commandments, including the sixth and ninth. He warns that nobody can transgress any of God's commandments at any time without the danger of committing mortal sin. However, in order for any transgression to be considered a mortal sin, the act has to involve the core freedom of the individual. Haring finds it hard to believe that the average Christian commits a mortal sin, even if the matter is serious, whenever he takes pleasure in sexual thoughts or whenever an engaged couple experience a degree of venereal pleasure through kissing or hand-holding.[17]

Haring admits to another possibility of parvity of matter

common to all the commandments. One can conceive of an act of relatively small matter at a stage in one's development. The same act could very well be considered serious matter after further growth and maturity.[18]

Haring states that neither of these approaches negates the importance of the act or the gravity of the matter. In his mind the gravity of an act is determined only in proportion to the actual development of an individual's knowledge and freedom, and to the extent that one's basic option is evoked.[19]

The Fundamental Option Theory and Objective Morality

Many contemporary moral theologians reject the traditional teaching that mortal sin is the deliberate choice of a single specified action. If the sinner died unrepentant, eternal damnation was his lot. Since the contemporary Catholic no longer experiences God as vindictive but rather as a friend, an intimate, a lover, John Milhaven believes that this has led to a new understanding of sin, which greatly affects the manualists' teaching on parvity of matter.[20]

Most contemporary moral theologians reject the traditional teaching which denies parvity of matter in sexual sins. The heavy emphasis on the subjective aspect of morality has lessened the importance of the objective in determining the gravity of a sin. Because of a new understanding of the natural law and the general acceptance of the fundamental option theory, most theologians admit the possibility of parvity of matter in sins against the sixth and ninth commandments.

Josef Fuchs is a strong proponent of the fundamental option theory. He does not specifically treat of parvity of matter in sexual acts. However, from his writings in the area of general moral theology one can deduce from his thoughts the possibility of parvity of matter in sins against the sixth and ninth commandments.

To begin with, Fuchs is highly critical of the physicalist mentality of the manualists and their predecessors. A study of man's biological nature does nothing more than give the manner in which nature operates as long as man does not intervene and the results one can expect of physical nature when allowed to take its course. Thus, in observing human nature, one can read nothing more than the facts to which the physical laws of nature pertain. To illustrate his point, Fuchs takes the example of rape. The physical law shows that rape may result in pregnancy and that such a result can be avoided by preventing ovulation. An analysis of human nature does not show which use of these physical laws is morally justifiable. Thus, one can see that correct moral behavior is not identifiable with conformity with physical nature as such. It is, rather, conformity with the human person taken in one's totality which includes human nature.[21]

In the context of morality, Fuchs does not consider human freedom subject to the physical laws of nature as such. On the other hand, these laws should not be ignored. Man should use these laws to develop himself and his world along humanizing lines. However, these physical laws do not determine the moral rightness or wrongness of an act. They are not invoked to regulate the free actions of an individual. Fuchs believes that the true measure of morality is <u>recta ratio</u> which understands the person in the totality of his reality.[22]

Fuchs does not believe that any one specific act of an individual can fully reflect one's totality because an act, which is performed in space and time, is governed by one's physical condition and efforts. In every moral act one must look to the extent to which one's personality enters into the act itself. The degree of good or evil in a particular act depends more on this than on the concrete nature of the act itself. According to Fuchs, it makes no difference whether the concrete nature of the act is serious or not serious, good or evil. That act is serious which emanates from and is imbued with one's personality. The execution of the act implements one's basic decision with regard to his fundamental choice of God or evil. Acts are considered light which are not imbued with one's personality and are not attempts at self-realization. They do not change one's fundamental choice, but they do incline one to change it.[23]

Fuchs does not completely abandon the material content of an action. In his opinion material content contributes something towards the judgment of an act's morality. To say the contrary is just as wrong as to say the human person is the only determinant. An individual cannot give to each action the meaning that appeals to him. The proper assessment of an act's morality depends on both the objective content of an action as well as the possible meaning for the person whether speaking of that objective content generally or in its concrete specific situation. Thus, for Fuchs the morality of sexual activity cannot be judged from the biological or psychological reality of sexuality alone. Nor can it be judged from one's personal experience alone. The morality of an act can be judged only from both aspects -- the meaningfulness of one's self-realization through a definite type of behavior in the sphere of biological and psychological sexuality. To put the question differently, "Where can one find the law engraved on the heart and the consequent will of God?" Fuchs responds that this law is not found in either the structure of the act or the behavior of the individual. Fuchs states that the will of God and the consequent morality of an action can be judged only from the total meaningfulness of an action centered in the concrete reality of the human person.[24]

To arrive at this total meaningfulness one has to have an <u>a priori</u> awareness of some of the essential elements of one's being, namely: one's own contingency and total dependence on an absolute, one's fundamental interpersonal individuality and corresponding social orientation to others, and, most especially, one's own personality, freedom, and responsibility. However, according to Fuchs even this <u>a priori</u> knowledge is not sufficient in itself. More is presupposed to arrive at the total meaningfulness of an action. One must have at least a vicarious experience -- a cognitive and affective awareness -- of what can happen to a person as a consequence of certain acts or patterns of behavior. One must experience vicariously and understand the world around him with its hidden possibilities. One must experience vicariously and understand the physical, psychological, and interpersonal consequences of certain behavioral patterns in the realm of such concrete reality. One must experience vicariously and understand the manifold significance of these consequences and the fact that certain realities and values are historically and sociologically conditioned.[25]

Human Sexuality

Since the main argument, used by the manualists in support of the traditional no parvity of matter teaching, was based almost exclusively on the procreative aspect of sexuality and very little on the unitive, it follows that any further broadening of the ends of sexuality or new insights into the meaning of sexuality would lead to a negation of the traditional teaching. According to Daniel Maguire, this is precisely what happened in contemporary moral theology. He states that one of the mistakes in the manualists' teaching on sexuality and also in the teachings of Vatican II was the notion that the ends of sexuality were competitively related and required ranking as primary, secondary, or equal. Maguire admits that sex is the obvious physical means of reproduction; however, this does not necessarily mean that sexual exchange should be ordered solely to reproduction. The needs of the community at large and other virtues might well indicate the opposite. On the other hand, he believes that the unitive aspect of sexuality is just as important as the procreative. Sex of its nature is unitive for all who participate in it. The intimacy of sex can lead to self-knowledge, trust, and friendship. Nature intends that both the unitive and possibility of procreation be aspects of sexuality, but according to Maguire this does not necessarily mean that they are conjoined in every sexual union.[26]

Charles Curran is highly critical of the manualists' methodology in the area of sexuality and especially of their stand in the no parvity of matter teaching. Their presentation of sexuality was over-emphasized and too negative. Contemporary theologians place the stress on love and service of one's neighbor as the identifying mark of the Christian. The anti-sexual prejudice of an older theology is being replaced by an appreciation of human sexuality in reference to the theology of creation, incarnation, and bodily resurrection.[27]

In Curran's opinion one very important obstacle to a proper understanding of human sexuality and its role in the life of a Christian is the teaching that all sins against sexuality involve grave matter. The negative attitude of pre-Vatican II theology towards sexuality accented the gravity of sexual sins. The presumption of the manualists that all complete sexual acts outside marriage as well as all directly willed imperfect sexual acts constitute grave matter is unfounded. The traditional teaching on the subject was due to an inadequate understanding of the natural law and an overstress in the area of sexual sins. The manualists' concept of the natural law distorted the real meaning and importance of sexuality because the manualists saw the sexual act only in terms of the physical/biological process. The psychological aspect of sexuality was practically ignored. Curran believes that the meaning of sexuality is distorted if one fails to give the psychological aspect its proper consideration.[28]

Curran also feels that the manualists failed to see the relationship between the person and one's acts in assessing the rightness and wrongness of an action. Vatican II calls for moral theologians to take the person as well as his acts into consideration. Pre-Vatican II theologians were more act-oriented than person-oriented. Curran believes that both the person and his actions must be considered equally in order to arrive at a balanced and proper understanding of the morality of sexual activity. One, for instance, should not consider sexual relations between a man and a prostitute, and a man and his fiancee under the all-inclusive term of fornication. According to Curran, criteria which are unable to distinguish the two acts are inadequate.[29]

Curran sees another difficulty in just concentrating on the physical aspect of a sexual act in determining its morality. An emphasis solely on the physical fails to allow for growth and maturity of a person sexually. In Curran's view, growth and development may present certain temporary problems along the way, for example acts of masturbation by a teenager; nevertheless these have to be viewed in relationship to the goal of an integrated human sexuality.[30]

Curran adds another reason why he believes that the manualists were held to teach no parvity of matter. Those who followed the traditional approach to moral theology taught that there was a close relationship between every sexual act and procreation, which they considered a very important value. Since they felt that every sexual act outside of marriage involves directly going against the procreation-education ends of the act, then it is not surprising that the manualists asserted the generic gravity of sexual sins. Contemporary moral theologians also admit the close relationship between intercourse and procreation. However, they do not see procreation as the only finality of the act. They cite recent documents of the magisterium, which omit identifying procreation as the primary end of marriage. Furthermore, even the approved method of rhythm indicates that not every act of intercourse is necessarily connected with possible procreation. Modern medical science supports their opinion. Scientists find that older biological notions exaggerated the importance attached by Catholic theologians to the relationship between sexual intercourse and procreation. Science shows that the vast majority of sexual acts do not result in conception. Thus, the importance of human semen is diminished since it is not the only active element in procreation. Curran concludes, therefore, that contemporary medical knowledge argues against the reasons of the manualists in assigning such generic importance to sins of sexuality.[31]

In responding to the 1975 Vatican <u>Declaration on Sexual Ethics</u>, Charles Curran expressly states that in his opinion there can be parvity of matter in sins against the sixth and ninth commandments. He does depart from the traditional understanding of objective morality. He considers the concept of grave matter only a presumption. It presumes that the matter in sexuality is of such importance that it will ordinarily involve a fundamental option and, thereby, break the relationship of love between an individual and God. The assertion that violations of the sexual order are always grave matter has no place in this contemporary understanding of human sexuality according to Curran. Why should chastity and sexuality be singled out? There are no other moral virtues in moral theology whose violation always involves grave matter. Curran believes that the traditional teaching of the no parvity of matter doctrine developed as a result of the Church's implicit ban of free discussion on the subject.[32]

Anthony Kosnik, William Carroll, Agnes Cunningham, Ronald Modras, and James Schulte in their work, <u>Human Sexuality</u>, begin their treatment of parvity of matter by criticizing the attitude of the Church toward sexuality. They feel that the teachings of the Church in this area prior to Vatican II were antiquated and inadequate. There was an over-emphasis on the procreative aspect of the generative act, which according to Kosnik and his co-authors greatly influenced the Church's understanding and teaching of human sexuality. Changes must be made. The modern-day Church must formulate a sexual doctrine that is faithful to fundamental values, and yet responsive to the changing historical, sociological, and cultural conditions in which it is taught.[33]

In laying the foundation for their theory of morality, Kosnik and his co-authors appeal to Vatican II as their starting point and, more specifically, to the urgings of the Council fathers that moral theologians open their minds to the findings of modern science. Christian moral principles and doctrine should be blended with the theories and recent discoveries of science. It is the task of contemporary moral theology to collaborate with the secular sciences.[34]

According to the authors of Human Sexuality, Vatican II's emphasis on the dynamic aspect of human nature as opposed to the traditional static understanding contributed greatly to the reformulation of traditional theological doctrine. The Council fathers viewed human nature as dynamic and relational, which is in keeping with the findings of contemporary psychology.[35]

Kosnik and his co-authors used Vatican II as their starting point because the fathers of the Council urged that moral theological speculation be necessarily and properly enculturated. In acknowledging the Church as an "historical reality", the fathers counseled the adaptation of Christ's message to the lives of all peoples. To bring about this adaptation, all must have a certain openness to the Spirit.[36] "With the help of the Holy Spirit it is the task of the entire people of God, especially pastors and theologians, to hear, distinguish, and interpret the many voices of our ear, and to judge them in the light of the Divine Word."[37]

With these thoughts as the cornerstone of their teaching, Kosnik and his co-authors turn their attention to the teaching of parvity of matter. They question the manualists' teaching which states that every willful enjoyment of venereal pleasure before marriage is a serious breaking of one's relationship with Almighty God. Such a teaching, they feel, must be re-examined. They question whether or not all sexual pleasure, even the slightest, is ordered by nature to the complete act of intercourse. It would seem at least possible that sexual pleasure can legitimately and wholesomely serve some other purpose. Kosnik and his co-authors question the validity of the manualists' fear that the propagation of the human race would be endangered by the refusal of many to enter the marital state, if venereal pleasure could be legitimately sought by the unmarried. They further question whether or not the sexual behavior of the unmarried should be evaluated in terms of physical pleasure as being the dominant moral factor. The authors feel that empirical evidence, history, and current theological reflection raise serious questions regarding the validity of many of these fundamental presuppositions.38

In order to free themselves from the confines of the manualists' understanding of human sexuality, the authors of <u>Human Sexuality</u> broaden the traditional formulation of the purpose of sexuality from merely procreative and unitive to creative and integrative. This concept -- creative growth toward integration -- expresses better the basic finality of sexuality. They feel that their formulation moves beyond the limitations inherent in the traditional procreative and unitive formula. Without excluding these ends, the creative/integrative formulation unfolds the fuller dimensions implied in Vatican II's statement that the nature of the human person and his acts constituted the harmonizing principle of human sexuality.39

Kosnik and his co-authors refuse to accept the manualists' understanding of the objective moral nature of a given act. They particularly reject the teaching which posits a meaning intrinsic to the very nature of an act -- a meaning that is absolutely unchangeable and in no way modifiable by extenuating circumstances or special context. Vatican II called for a renewal of moral theology in which morality is seen as a vocation, a way of life, lived out from the depth of a person's being. It is seen as a total response to God's love. It must not be reduced to a simple, external conformity to prejudged and prespecified patterns of behavior. Thus, Kosnik and his co-authors find that the evaluation of human sexual behavior, based on an abstract absolute predetermination of any sexual expression as intrinsically evil and always immoral, is woefully inadequate.40

However, this does not mean that they deny the existence of all objective criteria by which one can evaluate sexual behavior honestly. It is, according to them, possible and necessary to articulate some of the values which sexuality ought to preserve and promote. They feel that one can list certain values which are conducive to creative growth and integration of the human person. Sexual expression must be self-liberating. It must flow freely and spontaneously from the depth of one's being. This quality allows sexual actions to be a source and a means of personal growth toward maturity and rejects sexual expression that is self-enslaving. Sexual behavior must be other-enriching. It must have a generous interest and concern for the well-being of others. It must be honest. The depth of the relationship that exists between two individuals must be expressed openly and candidly. Sexual expression must be faithful. It must be characterized by a consistent pattern of interest and concern that can grow deeper and richer. It must be socially responsible. It must reflect not only individual relationships, but also the relationship and responsibility of an individual to one's larger community. Sexual expression should be life-serving. The creative and integrative should give witness to exuberant appreciation of the gift of life and the mystery of love.[41]

When such qualities prevail in acts of sexual expression, Kosnik and his co-authors feel that one's sexual behavior is wholesome and moral. On the other hand, when sexual expression is self-destructive, manipulative of others, deceitful, inconsistent, promiscuous, non-life serving, burdensome, and selfish, creative and integrative growth is seriously abused. The authors state that a much more sensitive and responsible method of evaluating the morality of sexual patterns and expressions can be reached by focusing on these values of wholesome sexuality and avoiding absolute categorization of isolated individual sexual acts.[42]

As in all theology, the truth of any theological teaching depends upon the validity of the arguments on which the teaching rests. If a particular theological teaching has no foundation in Scripture, tradition, or reason either explicitly or implicitly, then the teaching does not have much validity theologically. In the preceding chapters of this dissertation the theological arguments in favor of the traditional and contemporary teachings on parvity of matter were presented along with a historical background which contributed to a clearer understanding of the teachings. Before concluding this chapter, an objective criticism of the theological arguments upon which the traditional teaching on parvity of matter rests is in order. The results of this criticism will show that the teaching does not rest on solid ground. Contemporary scholarship points out that the manualists' use of Scripture, tradition, and reason do not support the traditional teaching on parvity of matter in sexual sins.

Those theologians over the centuries who taught the traditional teaching of no parvity of matter in sexual sins looked to these standard three sources to support their position -- Sacred Scripture, the teachings of the magisterium of the Church, and reason. For example, J. Aertnys, C.SS.R. and C. A. Damen, C.SS.R. cite three places in the writings of St. Paul which in their minds support the traditional teaching: Ephesians 5:3-5, First Corinthians 6:9-10 and Galatians 5:19-21.[43] Benedict Merkelbach, O.P. states that all sins of lust are serious matter ex toto genere suo because of the Galatians text.[44] H. Noldin, S.J. and A. Schmitt, S.J. also use the writings of St. Paul to support their stand on no parvity of matter in sexual sins.[45] Even as recently as 1979,

William B. Smith writes that Sacred Scripture leaves no doubt about the generic gravity of sexual sins. Besides citing the Ephesian and Galatian texts of St. Paul, he also indicates that Colossians 3:5 and Matthew 5:28 point to the gravity of matter in sexual sins.[46]

Even though Vatican II in the Dogmatic Constitution on Divine Revelation calls for a scripturally based moral theology by indicating that Sacred Scripture must be the soul of all theology, nevertheless most contemporary moral theologians and biblical scholars are very reluctant to cite any specific place in Sacred Scripture as the definite basis for an argument in support of a moral teaching. To do so is to ignore the principles of hermeneutics and to misunderstand the meaning and purpose of Sacred Scripture.

According to Josef Fuchs, S.J. when Vatican II mandated that moral theology be "more thoroughly nourished by scriptural teaching", it was not implying that this nourishment take the form of reference to specific places in Scripture in support of a theological teaching. The Council fathers certainly did not mean to imply that specific principles and a specific norm of morality could be found in Sacred Scripture. What was intended was that Sacred Scripture determine the fundamental orientation of moral theology.[47]

Contemporary moral theologians believe in the importance of Sacred Scripture for moral theology. Without the use of Scripture a moral theology will in time wander from the truth. Sacred Scripture is necessary if a moral theology is to maintain its Christian character. However, a scripturally oriented moral theology implies the proper understanding of Sacred Scripture in the light of modern scholarship and a proper methodology.[48]

Modern biblical scholarship has long since shown that the Bible contains no systematic theological treatise. Nor does it provide us with a developed theological system or synthesis of principles or precepts of Christian morality. Sacred Scripture certainly does not give solutions to the moral questions which have arisen over the course of time. On the other hand, the study of Sacred Scripture does not leave us empty-handed. It does provide moral theology with a general understanding of morals and guiding principles.[49]

The correct use of Scripture in moral theology requires a proper methodology. Josef Fuchs does not believe that the mandates of Vatican II in regard to a scripture-oriented moral theology are met by developing one or two biblical arguments or relying on a non-scholarly exegesis. The proper use of Scripture in moral theology does not mean a random choice of a few general texts or vague references. A scriptural proof that a certain action is sinful is not established by quoting a few texts which could possible imply such. Biblical exegetes hold that, if proof that a particular action is sinful is not clearly stated in the Bible, then one has to admit that biblical proof for the sinfulness of that actions is inconclusive. Fuchs believes that such a principle is true of all cases where the meaning of the text is vague or has a possible double meaning. This, according to Fuchs, is precisely the case with all the scriptural texts which indicate that unchastity (<u>porneia</u>) is sinful. The texts of themselves are too vague to prove this sinfulness. Since the term unchastity is too generic in meaning to employ Scripture properly in this instance, one has to show that unchastity has a particular meaning in a particular text. For example, to state that all extra-marital intercourse is sinful, one has to ascertain whether or not the text actually means that or whether or not only a particular form of intercourse is meant -- intercourse with a prostitute as in 1 Corinthians 6:12-20.[50]

Fuchs believes that exegesis is essential to the proper understanding of a scripturally based moral theology. Much more work has to be done by exegetes than put forth thus far. They have to tell whether or not those excluded from the kingdom of heaven as noted in 2 Corinthians 12:20, Galatians 5:20, and Romans 16:17 are so because of a "grievous" act. They have to tell us whether or not the exclusion results from every single grievous act or only when a habit has set in. Exegetes have to tell us whether certain norms, found in Sacred Scripture, must be considered as norms and principles or whether they are only the ideal toward which one should strive. Finally, exegetes have to help us distinguish between revealed principles and the personal opinion of the writer of the particular work. Fuchs gives as an example of this in St. Paul's views on homosexuality. According to Fuchs what St. Paul says about this should not be taken as revealed teaching but rather as Paul's thoughts which he expressed to contrast the life of the spiritual man with that of the carnal man.[51]

With this contemporary understanding of exegesis, it is very difficult to see how the traditional teaching on parvity of matter has any specific foundation in Sacred Scripture. The officials of the Sacred Congregation for the Doctrine of the Faith must have realized this since in their most recent document on sexual ethics there is no reference made to Sacred Scripture in support of the traditional teaching on parvity of matter.

Thus, it appears that the present teaching of the magisterium on no parvity of matter in sexual sins has no specific scriptural foundation. One could possibly argue from general principles; however, such an argument would be so vague and so forced as to carry little weight.

The Sacred Congregation for the Doctrine of the Faith in the 1975 Vatican Declaration on "Certain Questions Concerning Sexual Ethics" states that every direct violation of the moral order of sexuality is objectively serious. It further states that this is according to the Church's teaching. It is true that the magisterium has spoken on the question of parvity of matter in sexual sins. But it has not spoken conclusively, often, or very convincingly. With the exception of the direct affirmation in the recent Vatican Declaration, the magisterium has only spoken four other times on the topic.[52]

The first two times that the magisterium spoke concerning parvity of matter was during the reigns of Pope Clement VIII (1592-1605) and Pope Paul V (1605-1621). These two pontiffs ordered that those who taught that kissing for the sake of the pleasure experienced in it was not mortally sinful unless ordered to intercourse should be denounced to the Inquisition. The problem with this argument in support of the traditional teaching on parvity of matter is that no official record can be found of either of these Papal Bulls. However, this is not to deny their existence at some time. Sixteenth and seventeenth century theologians refer to them in their writings too often for them to be nonexistent. Thomas Sanchez, for example, refers to the two Pontiffs and their teaching in his *Opus Morale*.[53] The real problem with these Papal Bulls is not their existence, but rather their contents. Precisely what was condemned by the two Pontiffs is very difficult to find out. J. R. Connery, S.J. believes that, if the decrees actually condemned the teaching of parvity of matter in sexual sins, then there would have been no need for the prohibition by Claude Acquaviva in 1612. The degree of Acquaviva would have been superfluous, since the mind of the magisterium would have already been made clear in the Bulls. Connery feels that parvity of matter was not condemned by the two Pontiffs, but rather that kissing for the sake of the venereal pleasure experienced in it was not mortally sinful was the proposition that was really condemned.[54]

The third utterance of the magisterium in favor of the traditional teaching on parvity of matter in sexual sins occurred in 1661. The occasion concerned the question of parvity of matter in solicitation. The question was asked of the Holy Office whether or not a confessor should be denounced who was guilty of solicitation, even though the matter of the solicitation was slight. The Holy Office responded that in matter dealing with the venereal there is no such thing as parvity of matter and even if there was, it would not be present in this case. The confessor should be denounced and the contrary opinion is not probable.[55] This same response was later alluded to by Benedict XIV in the Apostolic Constitution "Sacramentum paenitentiae".[56] Connery feels that these two references at best indicate the mind of the magisterium, since in fact the opinion could have been rendered without necessarily referring to parvity of matter. On the other hand, since the question primarily concerns the matter of solicitation in the confessional, Connery believes that one cannot use the response of the Holy Office and the reaffirmation of Benedict XIV as a strong argument in support of the traditional teaching on parvity of matter.[57]

The magisterium spoke a fourth time concerning parvity of matter. In 1666, Alexander VII condemned the proposition which stated that kissing indulged in for the sake of carnal and sensual pleasure is only venially sinful, as long as there was no danger of further consent or orgasm, is a probable opinion. The proposition was the fortieth of forty-five which were condemned by the Pope. The condemnation carried with it an ipso facto excommunication, reserved to the Supreme Pontiff. Contemporary theologians feel that the probative value of the condemnation as an argument in support of the traditional teaching is not very convincing because of the wording. Connery believes that the statement of the propostion is too ambiguous. Does it include venereal pleasure or not? If it does, does the condemnation necessarily imply that other venereal acts, such as thoughts, looks, and touches, cannot admit of parvity of matter? Connery feels that the decree certainly condemns the complete act and orgasm as mortally sinful. Acts of carnal and sensual kissing in themselves are also condemned as serious matter. In his opinion this is the least one has to hold in the condemnation.[58]

The most influential voice in the development of the traditional teaching on parvity of matter was the Decree of Claude Acquaviva. Even though the Decree did not issue from the magisterium, nevertheless is deserves some comment because of its influence and because it certainly reflected the mind of the magisterium on the subject.

In April 1612, Claude Acquaviva, the General of the Society of Jesus, forbade all the members of the Society from teaching that some slight pleasure deliberately sought in re venerea could be excused from mortal sin. It forbade the members of the Society from espousing such a teaching under any circumstance whether publicly, or privately, or as probable, or even as tolerable. The Decree forbade Jesuits from even giving advice according to it. Acquaviva claimed that he arrived at such a decision after consultation with learned and authoritative Fathers in the Society because of the harm which the contrary teaching was causing to the Society and to the purity of life which the Society held in such high esteem for its own members and for those outside the Society. He felt that there was an inherent danger in teaching parvity of matter in sexual sins and he stated further that in reality it was morally impossible to distinguish between light and grave matter in the question of sexual sins.[59]

In a letter, which accompanied the Decree, to all provincials throughout the Society, Acquaviva expressed the hope that a more authoritative statement from the Holy See on the question would be forthcoming. He also noted in the letter that he based his expectations on the knowledge of Paul V's mind on the topic. He claimed that the teaching of parvity of matter in sexual sins was very offensive to the Pontiff.[60]

Even though the decree was quite general and ambiguous in meaning, still it played a very important part in the development of the traditional teaching. For all practical purposes it spelled the end for the teaching of parvity of matter. At that time in history, many educational institutions were staffed by Jesuits, who were forbidden under the strictest censure to teach anything other than the traditional teaching. Secondly, even though the Decree was not an official document of the magisterium, still the silence of the Church at that time in face of this decree, which it knew would have such great influence on the minds and spirituality of the faithful, has to be taken as approval of the teaching as presented by Acquaviva.

From the time of the condemnation by Alexander VII in 1666 until the Declaration on Certain Questions Concerning Sexual Ethics in 1975, the magisterium said nothing directly as regards the question of parvity of matter with the exception of Benedict XIV's reference to the Holy Office's Response in 1741 concerning parvity of matter in solicitation. This silence of the magisterium, according to Richard McCormick, S.J., is the strongest possible argument for the objective truth of the teaching, irrespective of any speculative proofs. In his opinion this silence indicated that the Church has herself over the years safeguarded the teaching, even though she has not explicitly condemned the opposite. McCormick stated that the Church as the guardian of morals has the obligation to suppress rigid as well as lax teaching. In matters of this kind if the Church were to espouse whether by affirmation or by silence a rigorous teaching which lacked objective validity, it would be rightly open to the charge of rigorism. This would certainly not be in keeping with the Church role as shepherd of souls, especially in this question of parvity of matter, since sexuality pertains so intimately to the daily lives of countless people.[61]

In 1975, under the auspices of the Sacred Congregation for the Doctrine of the Faith the magisterium spoke directly to the question of parvity of matter and reaffirmed the traditional teaching. The Congregation cited Christian tradition, the Church's teaching, and right reason as arguments in support of the traditional teaching. The document notes two utterances of the magisterium as evidence of the Church's teaching in this matter: the 1666 condemnation of Alexander VII and the encyclical letter, Humanae Vitae, of Paul VI. Neither reference treats directly the question of parvity of matter. Earlier in the chapter the ambiguity of the condemnation of Alexander VII in reference to parvity of matter was pointed out by John Connery. The reference in Humanae Vitae notes the beauty and the importance of the conjugal act and that the misuse of this act, even partially, contradicts the meaning and purpose of the act intended by Almighty God. Whether or not one can reason from this statement to a negation of parvity of matter in sexual sins is questionable. It seems, therefore, that the only solid argument which the Sacred Congregation has to support its position in support of the traditional teaching is the "mute" voice of the magisterium. It is reasonable to assume that the magisterium would not allow the teaching of the traditional position of parvity of matter, if it did not espouse the teaching.[62]

The theological arguments which the manualists and some contemporary moral theologians proffer in support of the traditional teaching are not very convincing. They can be reduced to three. Some theologians argue that the position of parvity of matter in sexual sins cannot be held because of the always present danger of orgasm. Noldin and Schmidt reject this reasoning. They feel that the so-called ever present danger of orgasm cannot be shown to be universally present in all. They cite the fact that pre-pubic youths and eunuchs can experience venereal pleasure without it being the beginning of an orgasm since they physically unable to produce sperm. The second argument from reason proffered over the years by those theologians who espoused the traditional teaching states that venereal pleasure of its nature compels one to seek the complete act, even though not originally intended. McCormick rejects this argumentation because it seems to contradict experience. In his opinion, the argument presupposes that the consent to the pleasure of the incomplete act cannot be separated from the consent to the pleasure of the complete act. McCormick believes that these two consents are really distinguishable.[63]

In his pre-Vatican II days McCormick held the traditional teaching on parvity of matter. In fact, he along with Josef Fuchs and J. Duhamel assigned the theological note of doctrina certa et communis to the teaching. McCormick and many of his contemporaries of that period reasoned that in every incomplete sexual act there is a violation of an essential order. They stated that every imperfect sexual actuation of its nature tends towards the complete act.[64]

This reasoning as put forth by many pre-Vatican II

theologians in support of the traditional teaching on parvity of matter is not convincing. One gets the feeling in this that the concept of no parvity of matter is already the fact and that reasons must be found to justify the objectivity of that fact. However, one cannot fault the manualists in this area. They felt that they provided a solid argument in favor of the traditional teaching when they stated that every degree of sexual actuation tends towards its completion in the sense that, once initiated, it has no staying power. The basic problem with the argumentation is that <u>gratis asseritur</u>. The manualists fail to prove that an incomplete sexual actuation has that determination towards completion. Secondly, the argumentation is contrary to experience. One can experience a slight venereal pleasure and take delight in it without seeking the total pleasure, even though conscious of the lack of complete fulfillment. Needless to say, if, as experience seems to testify, imperfect sexual actuation does not necessarily have to seek its completion, then it is difficult to see how the total malice of the completed act can be in incomplete sexual actuation. Secondly, even if one was to admit the argumentation of the manualists, the most that can be shown by their argument is that every incomplete sexual actuation is objectively evil. Whether or not the incomplete act admits of degrees of objective evil is not answered. Thirdly, in an effort to justify their argumentation the manualists point out other nonsexual acts such as perjury, blasphemy, and hatred of God also do not admit of parvity of matter because according to them each degree of the objective sin contains the substantial violation. If one does compare the matter of sexual sins with the matter of these other sins, can one equate the evil of a slight sexual glance with the evil of a so called light act of perjury, or blasphemy, or hatred of God? Fourthly, the argumentation seems to confuse parvity of matter with sexual actuation of the generative faculty. It is difficult to see how the argumentation would deal with slight sexual thoughts and fantasies, which may or may not involve any sexual actuation at all in the individual.

In summary, therefore, one cannot say that the mind of the magisterium in reference to the question of parvity of matter is not clear. In contemporary theology the Sacred Congregation for the Doctrine of the Faith addressed the question directly in favor of the traditional teaching. Even though this document is the only official word of the magisterium on the subject, still the mind of the magisterium concerning parvity of matter in sexual sins is certainly clear in pre-Vatican theology.

The response of the Holy Office in 1661 and the condemnation of Alexander VII in 1666 indicate the mind of the magisterium in this matter, even though the question was not directly addressed. The decree of Acquaviva, though only a private document, which proposed to give the official stand of the magisterium as regards parvity of matter in sexual sins, was not undermined or contradicted by the magisterium. Finally, for over three hundred years the traditional teaching appeared in theology textbooks and was taught by reputable moral theologians without any concern on the part of the magisterium. This silence in face of a question as serious as this indicates approval and support of the traditional teaching.

In this chapter we stated that moral textbooks prior to Vatican II taught that the goodness or badness of an act in the objective order depended on three factors: the act itself, circumstances surrounding the act, and the intention of the one who performs the act. In order for an act to be morally good, one of these three factors had to be good and the others at least indifferent. For an act to be considered morally bad, it was sufficient that only one of the three factors be evil. It is obvious, therefore, that in the teaching of pre-Vatican II moral theology, all three factors in themselves had the capability of being morally good or morally evil. In considering the matter of an act, there also existed the possibility of the matter of one act being more serious or less serious than another, depending upon the degree of disorder present in each act. There is, for example, less disorder in the act of stealing ten dollars from a rich man than in the act of stealing ten thousand dollars. Thus, in the manualists' understanding of morality, certain moral actions can admit of parvity of matter, others cannot.

As was stated earlier, many post-Vatican II moral theologians have swung away from the traditional teaching of no parvity of matter in sins against the sixth and ninth commandments. The emergence of the fundamental option theory of morality was the underlying factor for this break with the traditional teaching of no parvity of matter. Although the theory deals primarily with one's orientation to God, a graced existence, still the emphasis on a person-centered morality as opposed to an act-centered morality has repercussions even in the objective order of morality. Many post-Vatican II moral theologians question the validity of the manualists' triple font of determining the morality of an act. They question the validity of calling an act morally evil before considering the circumstances and the intention of the person who performs the act. Questions of this type have led some theologians such as Timothy O'Connell to identify motive as a circumstance and for all practical purposes state that the principal font of morality in the objective order is determined by the circumstance, and, more precisely, by the justifying or nonjustifying reasons for allowing the positing of the ontic evil, which is part of every human act. If this is true, namely that an act considered in itself, separate from circumstances is "moral-less" or premoral, then there can be no consideration of parvity or gravity of matter as the manualists understood the question. There can be no light or serious moral evil, if there is no moral evil present.

Before concluding this chapter, it might be well to point out some of the weaknesses of this premoral/proportionate reason approach to morality.

As one might suspect this contemporary approach in assessing the rightness or wrongness of objective morality has in recent years received a fair amount of criticism. The origin of this criticism comes from those traditional moral theologians who favor a deontological approach to moral norms and moral reasoning.

One such criticism centers around the notion of intrinsic moral evil. Traditional moral theologians have held that certain moral acts, such as abortion, contraception, sterilization, taking the life of an innocent human being, are intrinsically evil acts in the sense that no circumstance or no motive could ever justify them. Such acts are seen as evil through and through.[65] On the surface it seems that the contemporary approach to moral theology denies such a concept, since with a proportionate reason acts which were traditionally known as abortion, sterilization, contraception, and taking the life of an innocent human being can be justified. However, such is not the case. The proportionalists state that intrinsically evil acts do not exist on the premoral/ontic level, but only on the objective moral level. They do not speak of intrinsic moral evil until after the fuller and more concrete analysis of the moral act. Once it has been ascertained that there is no proportionate reason for performing an ontic evil, then those who espouse the premoral/proportionate reason approach have no problem with acknowledging the existence of intrinsically evil acts.

Another criticism leveled against the new approach to moral concerns the applicability of concrete universal moral norms. It seems that, since the morality of each act has to be judged in its concrete existing situation, there is no need for universal moral norms. The proportionalists respond that they have no problem with the basic principle of universal moral norms. They admit the validity of this concept, but they are more concerned with the acts to which the norms apply. Once an act is judged to be an objective moral evil, the proportionalists state that the act will be so whenever and wherever it occurs. They differ from the traditionalists in that they insist upon a more careful and more specific process of determining whether or not an action is objectively immoral.

Many traditonalists feel that the new approach of the

premoral/proportionate reason methodology leads to consequen-
-tialism or utilitarianism. The proportionalists answer that, if one considers the proportionate reason as a mere weighing or calculating of the harms and benefits in a given situation, then the new approach might well be branded as a form of consequentialism or utilitarianism. But this is not the case. The weighing procedure is not an adequate understanding of the notion of proportionate reason. The proportionalists see rather a more adequate picture of the situation. They look for what gives the action its meaning or its <u>ratio</u>. They look for that intelligibility which informs the so called material elements of the action. They deny that proportionate reason means the mere weighing of the good or bad results of an action.

Some traditional theologians have viewed and criticized the premoral/proportionate reason approach as being too subjective or individualistic, too little concerned with the community. The proportionalists see such a criticism as indicative of a complete misunderstanding of their position. They state that their approach insists on an objective moral order and they refuse to accept a form or intelligibility which cannot be substantiated in the premoral level of an action. Community and moral judgments have objectivity. An action does not become moral simply because someone thinks it is moral.[66]

Another criticism leveled against the proportionalist theory is that it tries to measure the unmeasurable. Since the premoral/proportionate reason approach is a system that depends on a quantitative summary of values, then determining the moral good becomes merely a quantitative process where one value is traded off against another. Such an approach leads to a disregard for the uniqueness and diverse kinds of value. If one fails to recognize the qualitative difference of values, then there is the distinct possibility of attempting to measure the unmeasurable. For example, can one weigh and measure the value of an unborn fetus, afflicted with Tay-Sachs disease, against other values such as the quality of life after birth, the burdens on the parents, the drain on medical resources?[67]

The most serious criticism against the new approach to moral concerns the action itself. According to Philip Keane this is probably the most vulnerable part of the theory. Keane states that the proportionists must develop a method which will determine which premoral features of an action are of such significance that they more readily lead toward an adequate moral description of the action. Some features of an action contribute more accurately to its objectivity than others. These latter can be considered extrinsic circumstances. Another problem with the action centers around premoral evil features. The question to be answered is which features of an action originate from human finitude and which originates from human sinfulness.[68]

1 Joseph Fuchs, S.J., "The Absoluteness of Moral Evil" in *Readings in Moral Theology No. 1.*, edited by Charles E. Curran and Richard McCormick, S.J. (New York: Paulist Press, 1979), pp. 119-120.

2 Edward Genicot, S.J., op. cit., pp. 32-33, pp. 114-117.

3 Joseph Fuchs, S.J., "The Absoluteness of Moral Evil," op. cit., p. 121.

4 Timothy O'Connell, *Principles for a Catholic Morality* (New York: The Seabury Press, 1978), p. 170.

5 Ibid., p. 80.

6 Philip S. Keane, S.S., *Sexual Morality: A Catholic Perspective* (New York: Paulist Press, 1977), p. 181.

7 Ibid.

8 Ibid., pp. 181-182.

9 Keane states that, to be morally significant, an ontic evil has to challenge a person in his or her moral decision-making process. Spontaneous instances of non-marital venereal arousal do not do this. Ibid., p. 225.

10 Ibid., p. 182.

11 Ibid., pp. 182-183.

12 Ibid., p. 183.

13 Ronald Lawler, O.F.M. Cap., op. cit., p. 210.

14 Bernard Haring, C.SS.R., *Free and Faithful in Christ*, Vol. 1 (New York: The Seabury Press, 1978), pp. 405-407.

15 Cf. Sacred Congregation for the Doctrine of Faith, *Declaration on Sexual Ethics*, December 29, 1975, n. 10: "Now according to Christian tradition and the Church's teaching and as right reason also recognizes, the moral order of sexuality involves such high values of human life that every direct violation of this order is objectively serious."

16 Bernard Haring, op. cit., p. 408.

17 Ibid., pp. 408-409.

18 Ibid., p. 409.

19 Ibid., p. 403.

20 John Milhaven, Towards a New Catholic Morality (Garden City, New York: Doubleday and Company, 1972), pp. 88-89.

21 Joseph Fuchs, S.J., Human Values and Christian Morality (Dublin: Gill and MacMillan, 1970), pp. 142-143.

22 Ibid., p. 143.

23 Ibid., pp. 45-46.

24 Ibid., pp. 146-147.

25 Ibid., p. 145.

26 Daniel C. Maguire, "Of Sex and Ethical Methodology" in Dimensions of Human Sexuality, ed. Dennis Doherty (Garden City, New York: Doubleday and Company, 1979), p. 127.

27 Charles E. Curran, Contemporary Problems in Moral Theology (Notre Dame: Fides Publishers, Inc., 1970), p. 159.

28 Ibid., p. 168.

29 Ibid., pp. 168-169.

30 Ibid., p. 168.

31 Ibid., pp. 169-170.

32 Charles E. Curran, Issues in Sexual and Medical Ethics (Notre Dame: University of Notre Dame Press, 1978), pp. 45-46.

33 Anthony Kosnik, William Carroll, Agnes Cunningham, Ronald Modras, and James Schulte, Human Sexuality: New Directions in American Catholic Thought (New York: Paulist Press, 1977), p. 78.

34 Ibid., p. 87.

35 Ibid.

36 Ibid., pp. 79-80.

37 Walter Abbott, S.J., and Joseph Gallagher, "Pastoral Constitution on the Church in the Modern World" in The Documents of Vatican II (American Press, New York, 1966), No. 44 p. 246.

38 Anthony Kosnik, et al., op. cit., p. 173.

39 Ibid., p. 86.

40 Ibid., pp. 88-89.

41 Ibid., pp. 91-95.

42 Ibid., p. 95.

43 J. Aertnys and C. A. Damen, op. cit., p. 434.

44 Benedict Merkelbach, op. cit., pp. 934-935.

45 H. Noldin and A. Schmitt, op. cit., p. 70.

46 William B. Smith, "Morality and Sexuality, What the Church Teaches" in Human Sexuality in Our Times, ed. Msgr. George A. Kelly (Boston: Daughters of St. Paul, 1979), p. 160.

47 Joseph Fuchs, S.J., op. cit., p. 26.

48 Ibid., p. 29.

49 Ibid., p. 28.

50 Ibid., p. 29.

51 Ibid., pp. 29-30.

52 Sacred Congregation for the Doctrine of the Faith, op. cit., no. 10.

53 Thomas Sanchez, Opus Morale, pars. 2, lib. 5, cap. 6, nr. 12, p. 45. "...namely, embraces, and libidinous kisses, even though the venereal pleasure, which is experienced in them, is enjoyed for itself with no reference to the act of intercourse, are mortal sins and to hold any position to the contrary is called by some temerarious and erroneous, which the Holy Fathers, Pope Clement VIII and Paul V, at present approved and ordered that those who hold the contrary be denounced to the inquisition.""

54 John R. Connery, S.J., op. cit., footnote 22, pp. 127-128.

55 "Qu: In solicitation must a confessor be denounced for parvity of matter? Resp: Since in sexual matters there is no parvity of matter, and, even if there could be, it would not be so in this case, it is agreed that the confessor be denounced and that an opinion to the contrary is not probable." Cf. H. Denzinger and A. Schonmetzer, S.J., Enchiridion Symbolorum (Freiburg: Herder, 1963), no. 2013., p. 448.

56 Ibid., p. 447.

57 John R. Connery, S.J., op. cit., p. 166.

58 Ibid., n. 2060., p. 454.

59 "Some members in the Society teach that in venereal matters a small degree of pleasure deliberately sought is not to be considered a mortal sin because of the smallness of the matter. At the very worst this can be very prejudicial not only to the reputation of the Society, but also to that purity of life which the Society tries to bring about in its own members as well as among externs. Because of the possible dangers to which such a teaching could lead and because of the moral impossibility of distinguishing on the practical level between light matter and serious matter, learned and respected fathers of the Society, with whom we have discussed the matter, judge the teaching to be altogether false, extremely dangerous, and certainly contrary to purity. Thus, after having given the matter serious consideration, we are forced to decree that no one in the Society, either publicly or privately, can teach parvity of matter in the future, not only as true or probable but not even as tolerable for any reason whatsoever. They may not indicate that the teaching is pleasing to them or counsel anyone in this matter." Rome 24 April, 1612, Claudius Acquaviva. As found in Ordinationes et Selectae Epistolae Praepositi Generalis Societatis Jesu, Vol. I, pp. 289-290. Unpublished manuscript quoted in Karl-Heinz Kleber, pp. 173-174.

60 John R. Connery, S.J., op. cit., footnote 2, p. 109.

61 Richard McCormick, S.J., Unpublished class notes on De Sexto Mandato, 1961. p. 50.

62 Sacred Congregation for the Doctrine of the Faith, op. cit., no. 10.

63 Richard McCormick, S.J., op. cit., p. 51.

64 Ibid., p. 49.

65 John R. Connery, S.J., "Catholic Ethics: Has the Norm for Rule-Making Changed?" in Theological Studies 42 (June, 1981): 247-248.

66 Philip S. Keane, S.S., "The objective Moral Order: Reflections on Recent Research" in Theological Studies 43 (June, 1982): 269-271.

67 Richard M. Gula, S.S., <u>What Are They Saying About Moral Norms</u> (New York: Paulist Press, 1981), p.97.

68 Philip A. Keane, S.S., op. cit., pp. 271-272.

Chapter V

A Critical Evaluation of the
Traditional and Contemporary Teachings
on Parvity of Matter in Sexual Sins

Throughout the many centuries of its existence, the magisterium of the Church has not hesitated to call certain moral acts evil in themselves. In recent times Vatican II has reiterated many of these morally evil acts. Such acts as infanticide, euthanasia, genocide, suicide, and devastation of entire cities with their inhabitants were considered by the Council Fathers as intrinsically evil acts.[1] Popes Pius XII[2], John XXIII[3], and Paul VI[4] taught that abortion was intrinsically evil. Paul VI stated that all means of artificial birth control were objectively evil.[5] Fornication, adultery, and sodomy were condemned by the Sacred Congregation for the Doctrine of the Faith.[6] Thus, the magisterium has consistently asserted its competency in designating certain acts intrinsically evil, even though others have questioned this competency.

In no area of theology has this exercise of power been so crucial pastorally than in the area of sexuality and, more precisely, in the question of parvity of matter in sexual sins. This is so because sexuality is such an intimate and important part of the human experience that any ill-conceived moral principle or prohibition concerning sexuality can greatly affect the attitude of an individual towards sex and, consequently, can have a very serious negative effect on the human and spiritual development of the individual.

In this chapter we will present some of the pastoral consequences of the traditional teaching on parvity of matter. At the same time we will also consider some of the possible pastoral consequences of the opposing contemporary teaching on determining objective morality and, more precisely, the pastoral consequences of teaching parvity of matter in sexual sins. Finally, we will attempt to present a way in which the magisterium could teach parvity of patter in sexual sins, while still employing the traditional determinants of objective morality.

Pastoral Consequences of the Traditional
Teaching of Parvity of Matter in Sexual Sins

The magisterium of the Church, as we have seen, claims the right to determine not only acts which are intrinsically evil, but also whether or not these evil acts are light or serious matter. Throughout the centuries, the magisterium has taught that some intrinsically evil acts can admit of degrees. Some of these acts can be light matter such as lying or stealing which, however, can become serious matter depending on circumstances. Others of these intrinsically evil acts admit only of serious matter as acts of blasphemy and the denial of one's faith.

Moral theologians in recent years have questioned not only the magisterium's right to determine certain objective acts to be evil in themselves, but also the magisterium's determination that a given human act is a mortal sin of its very nature. According to the manualists with some such acts there are no problems. They saw the fulness of evil in every part. Such acts as mentioned above -- the denial of one's faith and blasphemy -- are intrinsically evil acts to a grievous degree because the objects of these acts admit of no divisibility. In other words, to deny part of one's faith means the implicit denial of one's total faith, because the veracity of Almighty God is called into question. The same holds true for acts of blasphemy. One cannot vent one's hatred against Almighty God in only a slight degree. Either that hatred is totally absent from the act or it is totally present. In these intrinsically evil acts, pre-Vatican II moral theologians demonstrated that the total malice of the act is contained in every part of the act. Thus, in their minds there can be no parvity of matter in such acts.

In this dissertation we have considered the magisterium's teaching on parvity of matter in sins against the sixth and ninth commandments and the position of certain contemporary moral theologians on a new approach in determining the morality of objective evil. In this new approach the magisterium's right to declare an act intrinsically evil is directly challenged. Implicit in this challenge is a denial of the magisterium's traditional teaching on parvity of matter. The investigation of the subject in this dissertation has shown that the magisterium, except for one instance, has never spoken directly on the subject, but was content to allow theologians over the years to teach the absence of parvity of matter in sexual sins. It has also been pointed out in this dissertation that historically there have been certain events, one especially, which have prevented the proper theological development of the question of parvity of matter in sexual sins. This one especially historical event which greatly influenced and contributed to the formation of the traditional teaching on parvity of matter was the disciplinary decree of the General of the Society of Jesus, Claude Acquaviva, in 1612. The magisterium's stand in favor of the traditional teaching was also the result of its many centuries of over-protectiveness and its pessimistic overview of the true meaning of sex, stemming from the time of St. Augustine down through the ages.

In my opinion it is difficult to justify the magisterium's traditional stand on parvity of matter. It is very difficult to conceive how the malice in one brief fleeting erotic glance can be as grave as the malice in a brief fleeting blasphemous thought which the magisterium considers intrinsically evil. As was stated above, the object of a blasphemous thought is not divisible, whereas the object of a fleeting erotic glance seems to be divisible. From the very fact that the manualists distinguished between complete and incomplete sexual acts, it follows that these acts have a beginning, a middle, and an end. Since the alleged finality of all sexual acts, namely procreation, proper rearing of offspring, and an expression of love, is in no way violated in the incomplete act insofar as no orgasm occurs, it seems that the total malice of a sexual act cannot be present in any degree of the act short of the complete sexual act. To restate the difficulty in another way, if the matter in a complete sexual act is serious for the unmarried precisely because the ends of such an act, namely the propagation of the human race and the proper rearing of the offspring are not realized, it would seem that for matter in an incomplete sexual act to be considered grave the <u>finis</u> of the complete act would have to be achievable in every degree of the incomplete act. Experience shows that such is not the case. No theologian would say that the ends of human sexuality are found in such acts as unchaste looks or touches or in the desire for slight venereal pleasure, which stops short of orgasm. Since the ends of sexuality are not realizable in any acts but complete sexual acts, it is very difficult to see how the total malice of the complete act can be present in the incomplete act. Hence, the object of the sexual acts seems to be divisible.

Pastorally speaking, the traditional teachings of no parvity of matter in sexual sins, which developed partly in reaction to the immoral sexual practices of the Late Middle Ages and partly in the hope of promoting a greater respect among the faithful for the virtue of chastity, had many drawbacks. In this effort to preserve the dignity and beauty of sex, the traditional teaching, because of its emphasis on the negative, i.e., on the gravity of matter of sexual sins instead of the beauty and dignity of sex, gives the impression that sex is sordid. This traditional teaching with its emphasis on the negative is in keeping with a long tradition in the history of the magisterium's attitude on sexual matters. One author traces the roots of this negative attitude of the magisterium back through history to the teachings of the Gnostics. The Gnostics posited two co-equal principles of creation -- a good god and evil god. The good god was responsible for the creation of all spiritual realities such as the soul, whereas the evil god created all material realities such as the body. Because one's body was the creation of the evil principle, it and all its activities were considered evil. Thus, sexuality was identified as evil at the very beginning of Christian tradition.[7]

St. Augustine, who at one time in his life was a Manichee, did not do much to dispel this notion of the evilness of sexuality. At times, his Manichaean background surfaced in his writings as regards human sexuality. For example, he stressed the sinful aspect of sexual intercourse between married couples.[8] Augustine's negativism concerning human sexuality dominated the Christian scene for approximately the next thousand years until the time of St. Thomas Aquinas. St. Thomas had a positive attitude toward sexuality, but his treatment of the subject was not persuasive enough to offset the many centuries of negative thinking. Jansenistic thought did much to enhance and strengthen the negative attitude in Europe. This negative attitude was not confined only to the Roman Catholic tradition. Protestant Puritanism was an important factor in developing the negative attitude toward human sexuality in America. Thus, this long-standing attitude spans all sects of Christianity.

As one might suspect, this negative attitude, which the magisterium's teaching on parvity of matter exemplifies, has many ramifications in the faithful's understanding of human sexuality. Some of these ramifications are of a positive value, but others, though not intended, have had a devastating effect, especially in the area of marriage.

Most contemporary theologians agree that Vatican II played a significant role in reshaping the traditional role of human sexuality. The Fathers of the Council abandoned the older primary-secondary classifications of the ends of marriage to concentrate sexual morality on the love between husband and wife. The emphasis was shifted from a merely procreative aspect of human sexuality to an interpersonal meaning of human sexuality. The human element of love was seen because it flowed from one person to another through an affection of the will. Love was viewed as something that looked to the good of the whole person. Because of its presence in marriage, it enriches the expression of body and mind with unique dignity and puts a distinctive characteristic on marriage. The Council Fathers state that such love moves spouses to a mutual and free gift of themselves, which they manifest by gentle affection and deeds. Conjugal love far excels erotic inclinations, which quickly fade away. It is lasting and capable of great growth. According to the Fathers, the love between husband and wife "is uniquely expressed and perfected through the marital act." Such acts, by which the couple are intimately and chastely united, are noble and worthy as long as they are performed within marriage.[9] When these acts are expressed in a human manner, they signify and promote that "mutual self-giving by which spouses enrich each other with a joyful and thankful will."[10]

The problem with all of this is that the magisterium in

having sanctioned and sanctioning the traditional teaching on parvity of matter creates a totally different concept of love. Those acts which uniquely express and perfect the love between husband and wife and which contribute greatly to the growth and development of love within a marriage are considered and taught by the magisterium to be objectively evil before marriage, irrespective of any circumstance or intention of the agent. Such a position makes for many pastoral difficulties, which have disastrous results in the lives of married couples. In espousing the traditional teaching, the magisterium basically requires an attitudinal change on the part of an individual from before the marriage ceremony to after the marriage ceremony, if Vatican II's understanding of sexual love is to be realized. Because the magisterium teaches that the act of intercourse and other expressions of intimate affection are morally evil acts before marriage, and not only that they are evil, but also that they admit of no parvity of matter, this teaching could be interpreted as affirming that sex is sordid, forbidden, evil. After marriage the magisterium encourages married couples to enjoy the very acts which were interpreted as sordid, forbidden and evil; in marriage they suddenly become beautiful. Married couples are encouraged to engage in them to express their intimate love for each other. They are encouraged to enjoy the beauties of sex as a means of growth and development. The problem is, "Can one always make the required attitudinal change?" After years of experiencing the negative aspects of sex -- that erotic fantasies and actions are serious matter -- that fornication is an intrinsically evil act -- can one make the necessary adjustment in married life and use these same forbidden sexual acts as a source of beauty, of growth, and of union? It is certainly possible that many sexual dysfunctions among young married couples can be traced to the lack of a proper understanding of sexuality on the part of one or both partners.[11] The fact that a young man or a young woman has a wrong attitude towards sex and lacks this proper understanding of sex is due largely to the omission in their lives of proper sex education and to the magisterium's overall negative attitude towards human sexuality and most especially to the magisterium's espousal of such teachings as the traditional teaching on parvity of matter in sexual sins. In summary, it is practically impossible pastorally to counsel an individual who has been programmed to the intrinsic evilness of sexual acts at one point of his or her life to use those same acts at a later point in his or her life as a source of growth in marriage.

In this whole question of parvity of matter in sexual sins, there is a tendency among the faithful to identify the matter of a sexual sin with the sin itself. This obviously can cause great confusion in the forming of a conscience. How many times has one heard or read the advice of a spiritual director concerning the morality of a nocturnal emission? These over-zealous individuals would counsel that, even though no sin has been committed, still it would be better for the individual not to receive the Eucharist the following morning. Or, even though free consent is lacking in acts of nocturnal emission, and, therefore, no sin committed, nevertheless, it might be good to mention the fact of the emission in one's next confession. Such an attitude towards sex can certainly be attributed to this identification of serious matter with sin, which the traditional teaching on no parvity of matter might well have occasioned.

The traditional teaching on parvity of matter in sexual sins can have and most probably does have a serious effect on the lives of celibates, if one fails to understand the real meaning of the teaching. Since all sexual activity for the unmarried is portrayed as serious matter and since the magisterium, especially since the Council of Trent, has extolled the celibate state as superior in excellence over the marital state,[12] a celibate male or female has the tendency to ignore the affective development of his or her personality. The teaching engenders a great distrust of one's affective feelings. Such a person because of this alleged seriousness of sexual matter and the human proneness to sin has the tendency to be so protective of affections that he or she tends to avoid even platonic relationships with the opposite sex. One is constantly conscious of the ever-present specter of the seriousness of matter in sexual sins. Such an attitude, which results from an overall negative presentation of the true meaning of sex, can have grave consequences, for example, in the pastoral life of a priest. On the other hand, if that fear of sex, which the traditional teaching of parvity of matter has occasioned in the celibate over the centuries, could be alleviated by a reformulation of the traditional teaching, it would seem that his own affective development would grow and his effectiveness in counseling on sexual matters would greatly increase.

The traditional teaching on parvity of matter causes great difficulties for those who are afflicted with scruples or who have very sensitive consciences. Pastoral experience indicates that one of the primary concerns of scrupulous individuals is with "sins" of sex.[13] They identify the subjective with the objective order. Consequently, they see sin where there is no sin. They are not able to distinguish objectively serious matter from serious sin. Precisely because they cannot make that distinction, they identify purely natural looks and thoughts which are sexual in nature as mortal sin. Obviously, the traditional teaching on the seriousness of sexual matter plays havoc with the consciences of these individuals. It would be much easier for the counselor in dealing with the scrupulous to treat the matter in sexual sins as indifferent or, at the most, light matter. In promulgating the traditional teaching as it stands, the magisterium adds to the despair and forgets its role as shepherd.

In 1612, when Claude Acquaviva issued his decree concerning the teaching of parvity of matter by members of the Society of Jesus, one of the reasons he proffered for his prohibition was that he wanted to provide a greater inducement for the practice of chastity both in the Society and among externs. However, it seems that the traditional teaching favors just the opposite. That which the traditional teaching seeks to preserve -- a respect for chastity -- is precisely what is discouraged by the teaching. Why should one settle for less? Common sense would indicate that if a young, unmarried man, for example, is bent on seeking venereal pleasure, he might as well perform those sexual acts which will provide him with the greatest degree of pleasure, since the matter in every sexual sin according to the traditional teaching is grave whether the matter is a passionate kiss, or a fully completed act of fornication. If one should object by saying that this is not true because there is a greater malice in an act of fornication than in a passionate kiss, then it would seem that there could be grounds for lightness of matter in sexual sins based on whether or not one is dealing with a complete or incomplete act.

It is obvious in considering the effects of the traditional teaching on the lives of the faithful that it places an over-emphasis on sex in one's life. In espousing this teaching the magisterium emphasizes one human activity totally out of proportion when compared with the other human activities within the human person. The magisterium is also oblivious of the moral sense of the faithful in this area.

In speaking of the malice of masturbation the <u>Declaration on Sexual Ethics</u> states that the act is a serious intrinsic evil act. The writers of the document refer to the constant teaching of the magisterium and the moral sense of the faithful as arguments in support of the statement.[14] If the moral sense of the faithful is a valid source of determining the goodness or badness of an act as the document indicates, then using the same criterion, it would seem that the traditional teaching on parvity of matter in sexual sins is somewhat rigid. The moral sense of the faithful does not consider a fleeting glance at a partially clad woman or a brief lustful kiss even though done with sufficient reflection and free consent to be matter for confession. This moral sense seems to have the proper balance between such acts and acts of fornication and adultery, which the moral sense of the faithful considers serious matter.

It is evident, therefore, that the traditional teaching on parvity of matter was the result of a methodology and a culturally conditioned understanding of sexuality. Because of the mandate of Vatican II, which exhorts theologians to rethink and update many of the traditional teachings of theology, one hopes that the magisterium's attitude towards sex as manifested in the traditional teaching on parvity of matter in sexual sins will be one of teachings officially reconsidered. The magisterium's recent change towards a personalist attitude in reference to marriage is certainly a step in the right direction of understanding the proper role of sex in the life of a human being. This reconsideration of many past teachings on sex would free the magisterium of past prejudices and would lead to a better understanding and more positive outlook on sex. Some of the long-standing prohibitions of the magisterium in reference to sex brought about by an over-protective shepherd and by the fear of abuse would be eliminated. This reconsideration of the traditional teaching would allow such teachings on sex as the traditional one on parvity of matter to fall by the wayside and would rightly place the whole question of sex under the virtue of temperance which allows right reason to regulate the desire for pleasures of food, drink, and sex.

Pastoral Consequences of the Contemporary Teaching on Parvity of Matter in Sexual Sins

The traditional teaching on parvity of matter can have some positive benefits on the pastoral life of the Church. If understood correctly, it could generate a respect for the importance of sex. It could show that sex should not be used at one's whim. Another advantage in the traditional teaching is the security in knowing which acts are bad and to be avoided by the faithful. A third advantage consists in the uniformity in counseling which the traditional teaching provided. In other words, such acts as masturbation and fornication are evil for all irrespective of circumstance or proportionate reason. Many of these good effects which the traditional teaching on parvity of matter in sexual sins causes in the pastoral life of the Church will be lacking in the contemporary approach. Even though it is very difficult to point to any actual negative effects of the contemporary position on the personal lives of the faithful, nevertheless there are some potential problems which could develop in their lives. Given the background and the moral tradition to which the faithful have been exposed, it is possible to predict some of these potential problems, which will result as a consequence of the contemporary position.

One can certainly say that the contemporary position in determining the objective goodness or badness of matter is revolutionary, to say the least. It negates many of the moral axioms that were commonly accepted as valid principles by the faithful whether because of obedience or out of invincible ignorance. Still, these axioms played a very important part pastorally in the spiritual development of the faithful.

Prescinding from the question whether or not the faithful should be allowed to remain in their invincible ignorance, one can see that any denial of these important axioms or any new interpretation which differs from the traditional understanding will cause great confusion in their consciences. Such, for example, was the case when a young priest mounted the pulpit in his parish church to announce to the parishioners that every act of adultery was not necessarily a mortal sin.

A time-honored axiom which the contemporary approach reinterpreted and gave a new meaning to is "the end does not justify the means." Granted that the manualists were victims of their pessimistic understanding of sexual ethics, they consistently taught that a morally evil act can never be performed no matter what the reason or what the consequences, precisely because the act is evil. Contemporary theologians state, on the other hand, that no act is evil until the intention has been considered. The morality of an act is not predetermined. It is determined in part by weighing the consequences of an act and by the proportionate reason for positing the act. Thus, many contemporary moral theologians state that it is permissible to do an ontic or premoral evil to achieve a good end.

Such an approach to morality will have a great effect on the minds of the faithful. For years it was drummed into us that certain acts were always serious matter. Acts of masturbation, fornication, and adultery admitted of no exceptions. They were evil. These acts, joined with sufficient reflection on the part of the person who performed the act and with free consent of the will, were serious sins. As we have seen in this dissertation, the contemporary approach in determining objective morality holds that such is not necessarily the case. The intention of an act plays a very important part in determining that morality. However, this is not to imply that the intention of a particular act is the only determinant. Attention must also be given to moral norms and other aspects of life. The uniqueness of the moral agent, the moral situation, the comparison of present moral experiences with past similar ones, and the various values in conflict must all enter into the determination of objective right and wrong. The methodology of this contemporary approach tries to make clear the different options which deserve preference after considering all the values at stake. It tries to uncover the means proportionate to the intended good and the evil inevitably caused without losing sight of the agent and his possibility for growth. Man's judgment is at the basis of this determination. It seeks to determine whether or not there exists a proportion between premoral evil (disvalue) that is present in any human action and the good (value) that the individual intends. If a proportion exists and the good intended outweighs the evil that is present, it is a morally good act. Thus, in considering the determinants of objective morality in contemporary moral theology, the judgment about the proportion and the good that an action achieves is the essential element. A morally evil action is one in which there is no value proportionate to the disvalue produced. Only when this judgment is made, can an action be called a moral evil. Consequently, the intrinsically evil acts as traditionally understood by the magisterium have no place in the contemporary approach to moral theology.

Needless to say, this new approach in determining objective morality, which is the basis for the denial of the traditional teaching on no parvity of matter, calls for a complete reassessing on the part of the faithful of the objective morality of sexual acts, which they have traditionally believed to be seriously evil in themselves. Obviously, such a reversal of their thinking in this area will result in great confusion and disturbance in the consciences of the faithful. It will call into question the credibility of the magisterium which accepts the traditional teaching of the rigid stance of no parvity of matter in sexual sins. It could well undermine the faithful's confidence in the magisterium and cause them to wonder if, perhaps, the magisterium has taken a too rigid stance in other areas such as divorce and remarriage, women's ordinations, and celibacy. The same climate of uncertainty has long since occurred among some of the more learned faithful when the magisterium reversed itself by accepting the methodology of modern biblical criticism and by acknowledging the lack of inerrancy in Scripture.[15]

Just as the traditional teaching on parvity of matter exhibits a rigid approach in presenting the rights and wrongs of sexuality, so the contemporary approach could certainly be accused of causing a certain laxism in assessing objective morality. Since, according to the contemporary approach in determining the objective morality of sexual acts, the goodness or badness of an act depends on the good or evil consequences and on the proportionate reason for permitting the ontic evil in the act, there is the great possibility for an individual to rationalize moral evil out of existence. It takes a very mature and honest person to consider good and bad consequences without any bias especially when the pleasure of sex is involved. The same problem presents itself in deciding on the adequacy of the reason for allowing ontic evil. Theoretically, one might be able to judge a reason proportionate enough to offset the ontic evil in a particular act. However, in practice, an individual, affected by concupiscence, might well have the tendency to give oneself the benefit of the doubt to decide in favor of the pleasure. The obvious effect of this weakness on the part of the individual has disastrous consequences on one's spiritual development. We have a very similar situation in the area of sin when dealing with a person with a lax conscience. In this case, sin is often seen as nonimputable. In dealing with objective morality because of this possibility of self-deception and of a biased reasoning process truly evil acts are seen as indifferent or as good.

Thus, there are some advantages in specifying some acts as definite moral evils as in the case of the traditional teaching of parvity of matter in sexual sins, even though the unseen effects of such a teaching could be counter-productive to the total development of the individual. The effects of the traditional teaching in relation to the scrupulous and to the formation of a right attitude towards sexual acts in a person can be pointed out as examples of this counter-productiveness.

Because of this possibility of rationalization in the contemporary approach in determining objective morality and the "demoralization" -- the stripping away from human acts all the intrinsic moral good or evil found in them, one could experience a loss of respect for the virtue of chastity. It is evident that the traditional teaching on the gravity of matter in sexual sins separated sins against chastity from most of the other sins. This separation had the positive effect of engendering a certain fear of unchastity. It marked the virtue out as something special. This positive attitude is created in much the same way that the prohibitions against the taking of one's own life and against abortion implicitly create the positive attitude in an individual of a great respect for life. Even in wartime, soldiers who have witnessed death or have been forced to take a life often grow in this respect for life because they see the finality of death. This positive gain of respect for the virtue of chastity, which results from traditional teaching on parvity of matter in sexual sins, is less evident in the contemporary approach.

Because of this demoralization of "objective matter", which is part of the contemporary approach in determining objective morality, there is the possibility in the contemporary position on parvity of matter that the unmarried, especially the adolescent, might dabble a bit in the area of sex with the possibility of placing oneself in the proximate occasion of committing a mortal sin. In the traditional teaching on parvity of matter, since the matter was always serious, one would be counseled to drive immediately from one's mind all thoughts of a sexual nature, precisely because they are seriously evil in themselves. In the contemporary position, this immediacy is lacking, since the objective matter, considered in itself, is premoral or nonmoral. Thus, pastorally speaking, this contemporary teaching on parvity of matter could cause great distress and great confusion for those who are plagued with sexual problems and great temptations for the young, who out of curiosity are drawn to experiment in the area of sex.

Finally, the contemporary teaching on parvity of matter can cause great difficulty in counseling which was not present in the traditional teaching. In the new approach the uniformity of the traditional teaching is lost. As has already been pointed out, acts of masturbation, fornication, and adultery were evil for all under every circumstance. This is not necessarily the case in the new approach. What is considered light matter or even indifferent matter for one individual can be seriously evil matter for another, depending upon the evil consequences of the act and the lack of proportionate reason for allowing the ontic evil. For example, in the new approach the act of masturbation might be perfectly legitimate or only light matter for one individual because of the good consequences resulting from the act as opposed to the bad ones and because of the presence of a proportionate reason for acting in such a manner, whereas for another individual such acts could be evil because of the evil consequences and lack of proportionate reason, and thereby prohibited. Such a situation can cause great confusion for the counselee. To expose two individuals to the same "sexual matter" in the form of a physical act, for one of whom the act is serious because of a predominance of evil consequences and lack of proportionate reason, while for the other the same act could be light and not a moral evil at all, certainly exposes one to the charge of relativism or at least to the charge of discrimination. This lack of uniformity puts the counselor on the defensive in trying to explain when or whether a particular act may be performed.

Needless to say, even if the above criticism of the contemporary approach is valid, still one should not close his or her mind to this approach simply because of the pastoral problems which might result. The commonly accepted axiom, <u>the abuse should not prohibit the use</u>, is certainly applicable in the area of human sexuality. For example, if it can be proven that a traditional teaching of the magisterium such as the teaching of no parvity of matter in sexual sins is not only too rigid in its approach, but is also the product of a false methodology, then the pastoral problems that may result from remedying the situation must be considered necessary happenings. Truth must be sought whatever the consequences.

In summary, therefore, even though the contemporary approach to parvity of matter avoids many of the pastoral pitfalls of the traditional teaching, nevertheless it also has its shortcomings. The freedom which the new approach gives the possible individual is appealing, while, on the other hand, it does open the door to self-deception. It seems that, pastorally speaking, neither the traditional teaching with its rigid stance on the intrinsic evil of objective matter nor the contemporary approach to morality with its emphasis on the subjective is free of pastoral difficulties.

Obviously, any change in the teaching on parvity of matter will cause pastoral problems. Just the fact that the magisterium has given its silent approval and that the teaching went unchallenged for the most part through so many years are grounds enough to disturb consciences, if there is any attempt to reverse the traditional teaching.

On the other hand, I feel that the papal magisterium has the obligation to reconsider its position on parvity of matter in sexual sins, especially in light of Vatican II and the evidence presented in this dissertation. As has been shown, the papal magisterium has never spoken directly to the question with the exception of the 1975 <u>Declaration on Sexual Ethics</u>. Consequently, any reversal of the teaching would not be as traumatic to the faithful as it would be if the magisterium had taken a direct stand on the question, over a long period of time.

Many of the pastoral difficulties which resulted from the traditional teaching on parvity of matter, such as the difficulties in counseling the scrupulous, the psychological effects of the teaching on celibates, the mental gymnastics of reshaping the attitudes of newlyweds towards specific sexual acts, could be alleviated if the magisterium reconsidered its methodology in determining objective morality. It would also contribute to a more positive understanding of human sexuality. The past determinants of object, circumstance, and intention have led to much confusion and inaccuracies. For example, the magisterium has taught that such acts as masturbation, fornication, and adultery are intrinsically evil acts, as if only the moral object, the act in itself were being considered. This, however, is not the case. Acts of masturbation, fornication, and adultery are not strictly the <u>materia circa quam</u>. These acts are already "circumstanced." Thus, when the magisterium states that masturbation, fornication, and adultery are intrinsically evil acts and admit of no parvity of matter, it is basically saying that the act of arousal, which is really the <u>materia circa quam</u>, and the added circumstance are evil in themselves. Obviously, this is not true. The act of sexual arousal cannot be considered intrinsically evil because it is a natural phenomenon, as witnessed in any marriage situation. It is necessary, therefore, that the magisterium be very specific in what it includes in the act in its narrowest and strictest sense before any new direction can be formulated in this area of parvity of matter.

Richard McCormick is in total agreement with the revision of the traditional methodology in determining objective morality precisely because of the confusion that results from it. He feels that the magisterium has been inconsistent in the exercise of that methdology in human sexuality. To point up that inconsistency, he cites the treatment of theft and sexual acts as examples. The magisterium defines theft not only as taking what belongs to another, but also as being against the will of the owner. According to McCormick, this latter part of the definition is a circumstance. It is included in the definition as essential to the act and excludes the possibility of any exceptions. However, in dealing with sexual acts the magisterium sees things differently. She treats an act of fornication, adultery, and masturbation, which are in reality a combination of matter and circumstance, as constituting the matter by itself.[16]

One immediate gain from this reassessment of her methodology would be liberating the process of sexual arousal from its evil and sinful connotation. Of itself, sexual arousal is nonmoral or premoral. It is neither good nor bad. If such a point could be taught in sex education classes, then the attitudinal change, which is required as a result of the traditional teaching on parvity of matter because of the identification of object and circumstance, would not be necessary, since sexual arousal is quite natural, even involuntary at times, and is good or evil depending on circumstance. Granted that the magisterium never actually taught that sexual arousal of itself was intrinsically evil, nevertheless, by treating the act and the circumstance as one, the inference was certainly easily deduced.

Pre-Vatican II moralists cite St. Thomas as their authority in assigning moral goodness or badness to an external act.[17] However, St. Thomas, himself, would not concur. He held for the nonmoral character of the external act. He did not see how an act could be evaluated morally without taking into consideration the subject and the reason for positing the action. In his mind an act of itself was nothing more than an abstraction to which a moral evaluation cannot be applied. Even though the exterior act is different from the interior act, still they must be considered as one act when one determines their morality. It is the inner act of the will which directs the exterior act towards its end and that makes it a concrete human act. St. Thomas feels that it is only the concrete totality that has moral meaning, not a part of the totality, which the magisterium employs in designating certain acts intrinsically evil. It is the motive or reason of the individual for placing the act, which specifies the act.[18] Thus, for St. Thomas, many acts can appear the same exteriorly, but the morality of the acts can vary, depending upon the end to which the will directs the exterior action.[19]

Scrupulous individuals would also benefit greatly from such a precision. If they could be convinced that sexual arousal of itself is not intrinsically evil, they would be relieved of much anxiety and fear. That tendency of identifying objective evil with sin would be taken away. This would give the counselor or the priest-confessor a positive base from which to start. It is almost an impossible task to teach a scrupulous person the distinction between objective evil and sin.

The abolishment of the concept of intrinsically evil acts would surely lead to a more positive attitude towards sex among celibates. It would allow them to look at sex more realistically. The question of the morality of nocturnal emission would not even be matter for moral theology, much less matter for confession.

On the supposition that the magisterium made this precision between object and circumstance and opted for the nonmoral character of the act of itself, then the further question remains: could one teach that in sexual sins there could be parvity of matter?

I believe that the magisterium could teach parvity of matter in sexual sins, if the notion of circumstance was included in the understanding of matter. Since it is the circumstance (and I include in this understanding of circumstance the motive or the end of the act) that in reality determines the morality of the act, it seems that it can also be the determinant of the gravity or the lack of gravity of a particular act. The question of theft as treated in the traditional moral manuals is evidence of the fact that the notion of circumstance can determine the gravity or lightness of matter in acts of theft. As has been already pointed out, to steal ten dollars from a rich man is only light matter, whereas to steal the same sum from a pauper is serious matter.

This influence of circumstance in determining the gravity or lightness of matter is also apparent in assessing the morality of sexual sins. The moral manuals list acts of fornication, adultery, masturbation, and bestiality as evil because they all involve sexual arousal. Nevertheless, each act is progressively worse than the other because an added circumstance increases the gravity of the matter.

Thus, this idea of circumstance adding to or subtracting from the gravity or lightness of the matter is not a product of contemporary theologizing. It has a place in the tradition of moral theology. Circumstances are a determinant of the morality of an act. They can also determine the gravity or lightness of the act.

There can be no doubt that Vatican II moved away from a classicist methodology to a historically conscious methodology in theology. It is also evident that it moved away from a biologism-type moral theology to a person-centered moral theology. With these changes in mind it seems that Vatican II has opened the door for a rethinking of past teachings on sexuality, especially in regard to the traditional teaching on parvity of matter. As we have seen in this dissertation, the magisterium approved of this teaching because it primarily saw the connection between sexual arousal and procreation. Since Vatican II pointed up the other ends of sexuality without declaring any hierarchy among them, the main argument in support of the traditional teaching loses its validity.

Taking matter to include both act and circumstance, one can see the possibility of parvity of matter in sexual sins. For example, there are certainly grounds for a distinction between serious and light matter in the case of sexual intercourse between a man and a prostitute and between an engaged couple who two weeks before their marriage use the act to express their true love for each other. One finds it difficult in comparing the matter of both situations to say they are equally evil. It would seem that the commitment of the engaged couple toward each other could allow for parvity of matter.

The same procedure holds for determining the gravity or lightness of the matter of masturbation. Anthony Kosnik and his co-authors list a variety of acts of masturbation -- adolescent masturbation, compensatory masturbation, masturbation of necessity, pathological masturbation, medically indicated masturbation, and hedonistic masturbation.[20] To list all these acts as serious matter is to ignore completely the circumstance of each act. One finds it difficult to put medically indicated masturbation or pathological masturbation in the same category of gravity as hedonistic masturbation. Thus, it seems that the magisterium could teach parvity of matter by just considering acts of human sexuality in their concrete totality.

Earlier in this dissertation we pointed out that St. Augustine allowed for the circumstance to lessen the evil of the act. He cited the example of a wife whose husband was in serious debt and in danger of being incarcerated in debtor prison. The man to whom the money was owed took a fancy to the debtor's wife and offered to release the husband from his debt if she had sexual relations with him. Unwilling as she was, she satisfied the man's desire. Augustine did not look upon this act as serious because the circumstance determined the degree of malice of the matter.[21] Modern day theologians discuss a similar case of a woman in a concentration camp. She could secure her release and return to her husband and children if she became pregnant in prison. To accomplish this, she had sexual relations with a guard. Many contemporary moral theologians would not consider her act evil and certainly not gravely evil.[22]

In conclusion, it would seem that the magisterium could reverse its traditional stand and acknowledge parvity of matter in sexual sins by rethinking its teaching on intrinsically evil matter and by broadening the notion of matter to include both the premoral act and attending circumstances. Vatican II mandates that religious practice and morality keep pace with the findings of modern day science and an ever-advancing technology. This requires that the magisterium study data from theological, philosophical, and psychological anthropology. The new findings in these sciences have shed new light on the meaning and understanding of man's nature and his acts. In light of this new understanding, many of the traditional teachings of the magisterium will have to be rethought and changed, if they are to have any validity in the modern world.

1 Vatican II, "Gaudium et Spes" in The Documents of Vatican II, op. cit., 27, 51, 79, 80.

2 Pius XII, "Address to the Italian Medical-Biological Union of St. Luke: in Love and Sexuality, ed. Odile Lilbard (Wilmington, North Carolina: McGrath and Company, 1978), pp. 91-92.

3 John XXIII, "Mater et Magistra" in Acta Apostolicae Sedis 53 (1961), 194.

4 Paul VI, "Address to the Society of Italian Catholic Jurists" in Love and Sexuality, op. cit., p. 390.

5 Paul VI, "Humanae Vitae" in Acta Apostolicae Sedis 60 (1968), 14.

6 Sacred Congregation for the Doctrine of the Faith, op. cit., 7, 8.

7 Philip S. Keane, S.S., Sexual Morality: A Catholic Perspective, op. cit., pp. 5-9.

8 St. Augustine, City of God, Book 14, Chapters 16-27.

9 Vatican II, " Pastoral Constitution on the Church in the Modern World" in The Documents of Vatican II, op. cit., pp. 252-253.

10 Ibid., p. 253.

11 Fred Belliveau and Lin Richter, Understanding Human Sexual Inadequacy (Little, Brown and Company, Boston, 1970), pp. 162-164.

12 Cf. DB. 980. "If anyone should say that the conjugal state is a higher state than that of virginity or celibacy, and that it is not better and more blessed to remain in the state of virginity or celibacy than to marry, let him be anathema" and cf. Pius XII, "Sacra Virginitas" in Acta Apostolicae Sedis, Vol. 46 (1954), pp. 170 and 174.

13 Dr. Andre' Lauras, "The Scrupulous and the Obsessed" in The Treatment of Scruples, edited and translated by Malachy G. Carroll (Divine Word Publications, Techny, Ill., 1964), p. 55.

14 Sacred Congregation for the Doctrine of the Faith, Declaration of Sexual Ethics, n. 9.

15 Raymond E. Brown, *Biblical Reflections on Crises Facing the Church* (Paulist Press, New York, 1975), pp. 111-116.

16 Richard A. McCormick, S.J., "Notes on Moral Theology" in *Theological Studies* 36 (1975) pp. 88-89.

17 St. Thomas Aquinas, *Summa Theologica*, I-II, 18,3.

18 "The end insofar as it pre-exists in the mind does pertain to the will. And in this way it does specify the human or moral act." *Summa Theologica*, I-II, 1, 3. ad 2.

19 "And for that reason nothing prevents acts which are the same according to their species of nature from being different according to their moral species, and vice versa." Ibid., ad. 3.

20 Anthony Kosnik et al, *Human Sexuality*, op. cit., pp. 226-228.

21 St. Augustine, *De Sermone Domini in Monte*, PL 34, 1254. Even though St. Augustine does not explicitly state that the woman was not guilty of adultery, it certainly is inferred from what he writes. D. Prummer paraphrases Augustine as follows: he "does not dare to define that these spouses sinned, and he permits everyone to think what he will since these spouses 'in no way judged that in these cirumstances that act was adultery' " D. Prummer, *Manuale Theologiae Moralis* (Friburgi Brisgoviae: Herder and Co., 1935), 1, 111, 1.

22 Dennis Doherty, "The Tradition in History", op. cit., p. 60.

Bibliography

1. Primary Sources

   A. Earlier Theologians

   Aquinas, St. Thomas. Quaestiones Disputatae:
       De Malo. Vol. II. Augustae Taurinorum, 1914.
   ------. Scriptum Super Libros Sententiarum.
       Paris, 1929.
   ------. Summa Contra Gentiles. Edited by C. Pera,
       P. Marx, and P. Caramello. Turin-Rome, 1961.
   Augustine, St. City of God. Book 14.
   Azpilcueta, Martinus de. Opera omnia in quinque
       tomos divisa. Venice, 1601.
   Billuart, O.P., Charles-Rene'. Summa S. Thomae
       hodiernis academiarum moribus accomodata cursus
       theologiae universalis. Wirceburgii, 1758.
   Caramuel, Juan. Commentarius in Regulam
       D. Benedicti. Bruges, 1640.
   ------. Theologia Moralis Fundamentalis. Lyons, 1675.
   Cardenas, S.J., Juan de. Crisis Theologica.
       Venice, 1710.
   Lacroix, S.J., Claudius. Theologia Moralis.
       Venice, 1725.
   Lehmkuhl, Augustinus. Theologia Moralis.
       Edition 10. Frieburg: Herder, 1902.
   Liguori, C.SS.R., Alphonsus. Theologia Moralis.
       Antwerp: Jassens and Van Merlen, 1821.
   Magister, Martinus. Quaestiones Morales. Tom. 1:
       De Temperantia cum virtutibus adnexis.
       Paris, 1490.
   Migne, J.P. Patrologiae Cursus Completus Series
       Latina. 221 Volumes. Paris, 1844-1864.
   Sanchez, Thomas. De Matrimonio. Venice, 1606.
   ------. Opus Morale. Venice, 1622.

   B. Manualists

   Aertnys, C.SS.R., J. and Damen, C.SS.R., C.A.,
       Theologia Moralis. Turin: Marietti, 1939.
   Davis, S.J., Henry. Moral and Pastoral Theology.
       Vol. 2. New York: Sheed and Ward, 1935.
   Genicot, S.J., Edward. Theologiae Moralis
       Institutiones. Brussels: A. Dewit, 1909.
   Merkelbach, O.P., Benedict H. Summa Theologiae
       Moralis. 5th ed. Vol. II. Paris:
       Desclee De Brouwer et Soc., 1946.
   Noldin, S.J., H. and Schmitt, S.J., A. Summa
       Theologiae Moralis: De Sexto Praecepto et De
       Usu Matrimonii. Innsbruck: F. Rauch, 1934.

C. Contemporary Authors

Curran, Charles E. "Absolute Norms and Medical Ethics." In *Absolutes in Moral Theology?* Edited by Charles E. Curran. Washington, D.C.: Corpus Instrumentorum, Inc., 1968.

------. *A New Look at Christian Morality.* Notre Dame: Fides Publishers, Inc., 1968.

------. *Issues in Sexual and Medical Ethics*, Notre Dame: University of Notre Dame Press, 1978.

------. *Transition and Tradition in Moral Theology.* Notre Dame: University of Notre Dame Press, 1979.

Fuchs, S.J., Joseph. *De Castitate et Ordine Sexuali.* Roma: Pontificia Universitas Gregoriana, 1960.

------. *Human Value and Christian Morality.* Dublin: Gill and Macmillan, 1970.

------. "The Absoluteness of Moral Terms." In *Readings in Moral Theology No. 1; Moral Norms and Catholic Tradition*, pp. 94-137. Edited by Charles E. Curran and Richard McCormick, S.J. New York: Paulist Press, 1979.

------. *Theologia Moralis Generalis.* Roma: Pontificia Universitas Gregoriana, 1960.

Haring, C.SS.R., Bernard. *The Law of Christ.* Translated by Edwin G. Kaiser. Westminster, Md.: Newman Press, 1961.

------. *Toward a Christian Moral Theology.* Notre Dame: University of Notre Dame Press, 1966.

------. *Morality is for Persons.* New York: Farrar, Straus and Giroux, 1971.

------. *Free and Faithful in Christ.* 3 vols. New York: The Seabury Press, 1978

Keane, S.S., Philip S. *Sexual Morality: A Catholic Perspective.* New York: Paulist Press, 1977.

Kleber, Karl-Heinz. *De Parvitate Materiae in Sexto.* Regensburg: Verlag Friedrich Pustet, 1971.

Kosnik, Anthony; Carroll, William; Cunningham, Agnes; Modras, Ronald; and Schulte, James. *Human Sexuality: New Directions in American Catholic Thought.* New York: Paulist Press, 1977.

McCormick, S.J., Richard A. *Notes on Moral Theology: 1965 through 1980.* Washington, D.C., The University Press of America, 1981.

------. "Intrinsic Evil, Moral Norms, and the Magisterium" in Notes on Moral Theology: 1982. *Theological Studies* (March, 1983): 71-86.

Monden, S.J., Louis, *Sin, Liberty and Law.* New York: Sheed and Ward, 1965.

D. General

Acta Apostolicae Sedis Commentarium Officiale. Romae, 1909.

Archivum Romanum Societatis Jesu. Ordinationes et Selectae Epistolae Praepositi Generalis Societatis Jesu. Rome.

Codex Juris Canonici. Westminster: The Newman Press, 1961.

Denziger, H. and Schoenmetzer, A. Enchiridion Symbolorum. Freiburg: Herder, 1962.

New Catholic Encyclopedia. 17 volumes. New York: McGraw-Hill, 1966.

Sacred Congregation for the Doctrine of the Faith. Declaration on Certain Questions Concerning Sexual Ethics. December 29, 1975. AAS 68 (1976), 77-96.

II. Secondary Sources

A. Books

Adam, August. The Primacy of Love. Translated by Elizabeth C. Noonan. Cork, Ireland: The Mercier Press Limited, 1957.

Belliveau, Fred and Richter, Lin. Understanding Human Sexual Inadequacy. Boston: Little, Brown and Company, 1970.

Brown, Raymond E. Biblical Reflections on Crises Facing the Church. New York: Paulist Press, 1975.

Curran, Charles E. and McCormick, S.J., Richard A. Readings in Moral Theology No. 1: Moral Norms and Catholic Tradition. New York: Paulist Press, 1979.

------. Readings in Moral Theology No. 2: The Distinctiveness of Christian Ethics. New York: Paulist Press, 1980.

------. Readings in Moral Theology No. 3: The Magisterium and Morality. New York: Paulist Press, 1982.

Dedek, John F. Contemporary Sexual Morality. Kansas City: Sheed, Andrews and McMeel, Inc., 1971.

Doherty, Dennis. The Sexual Doctrine of Cardinal Cajetan. Regensburg: Verlag Friedrich Pustet, 1966.

Fagan, S.J., Sean. Has Sin Changed? Garden City, New York: Image Books, 1979.

Gula, S.S., Richard M. What Are They Saying About Moral Norms? New York: Paulist Press, 1982.

Jone, O.F.M. Cap., Heribert. *Moral Theology*.
    Translated by Urban Adelman, O.F.M. Cap.
    Westminster, Maryland: The Newman Press, 1960.

John XXIII. "Mater et Magister." Encyclical Letter
    of May 15, 1961. *AAS* 53 (1961), 401-464.

Maguire, Daniel. *The Moral Choice*. Garden City:
    New York: Doubleday and Company, 1978.

Manya, Joannes B. *Theologumena*. Vol. 1. *De ratione peccati poenam inducentis*. Barcelona:
    Duran and Bas, 1947.

May, William E. *Becoming Human*. Dayton, Ohio: Pflaum
    Publishing Company, 1979.

------. *Human Experience*. Chicago: Franciscan Herald
    Press, 1977.

------. *The Nature and Meaning of Chastity*.
    Chicago: Franciscan Herald Press, 1976.

Meier, Anton Meinrad. *Das Peccatum Mortale ex Toto Genere Suo*. Regensburg: Verlag Friedrich
    Pustet, 1966.

Milhaven, John. *Toward a New Catholic Morality*.
    Garden City, New York: Doubleday and Company, 1972.

O'Connell, Timothy E. *Principles for a Catholic Morality*. New York: The Seabury Press, 1978.

O'Neil, Robert P. and Donovan, Michael A. *Sexuality and Moral Responsibility*. Washington, D.C.:
    Corpus Instrumentorum, Inc., 1968.

Paul VI. "Humanae Vitae." Encyclical letter of
    July 25, 1968. *AAS* 60 (1968), 481-503.

Pius XII. "Casti Connubii." Encyclical letter of
    December 31, 1930. *AAS* 22 (1930), 539-592."

------. "Sacra Virginitas." Encyclical letter of
    March 25, 1954. *AAS* 44 (1954) 163-184.

Regan, C.M., George M. *New Trends in Moral Theology*.
    New York: Newman Press, 1971.

Schuller, S.J., Bruno. *Gesetz und Freiheit*. Dusseldorf:
    Patmos: Verlag, 1966.

van der Marck, William. *Love and Fertility*. London:
    Sheed and Ward, 1965.

von Hildebrand, Dietrich. *Ethics*. Chicago:
    Franciscan Herald Press, 1972.

B. Articles

Connery, S.J., John R., "Catholic Ethics: Has the Norm for Rule-Making Changed?" *Theological Studies* 42 (June, 1981): 232-250.

Doherty, Dennis. "Sexual Morality: Absolute or Situational?" *Continuum* 5 (Summer, 1967): 235-253.

------. "The Tradition in History." In <u>Dimensions of Human Sexuality</u>. pp. 39-78. Edited by Dennis Doherty. Garden City, New York: Doubleday and Company, 1979.

Glaser, S.J., John W. "Transition between Grace and Sin: Fresh Perspectives." <u>Theological Studies</u> 29 (June, 1968): 260-274.

Grisez, Germain. "The Roots of the New Morality." <u>Homiletic and Pastoral Review</u> 75 (June, 1975): 20-32.

Janssens, Louis. "Ontic Evil and Moral Evil." In <u>Readings in Moral Theology, No. 1: Moral Norms and Catholic Tradition</u>, pp. 40-93. Edited by Charles E. Curran and Richard McCormick, S.J. New York: Paulist Press, 1979.

Jennings, Theodore W. "Theological Perspectives on Sexuality." <u>Journal of Pastoral Care</u> 33 (March, 1979): 3-16.

Johann, S.J., Robert O. "Responsible Parenthood: A Philosophical View." <u>Proceedings of the Catholic Theological Society of America</u> 20 (1965): 115-128.

Keane, S.S., Philip S., "The Objective Moral Order: Reflections on Recent Research." <u>Theological Studies</u> 43 (June, 1982): 260-278.

Lawler, O.F.M. Cap., Ronald. "The Love of God and Mortal Sin." In <u>Principles of Catholic Moral Life</u>, pp. 193-219. Edited by William May. Chicago: Franciscan Herald Press, 1980.

Lonergan, S.J., Bernard J. "Cognitional Structure." <u>Collection</u>: Papers by Bernard Lonergan, 21-239. Edited by F. E. Crowe. New York: Herder and Herder, 1967.

------. "The Transition from a Classicist World View to Historical Mindedness." In <u>Law for Liberty</u>, pp. 126-133. Edited by J. Biechler. Baltimore: Helicon Press, 1967.

Maguire, Daniel C. "Of Sex and Ethical Methodology." In <u>Dimensions of Human Sexuality</u>. pp. 125-148. Edited by Dennis Doherty. Garden City: New York: Doubleday and Company, 1979.

------. "Moral Absolutes and the Magisterium." In <u>Absolutes in Moral Theology</u>?, pp. 57-107. Edited by Charles E. Curran. Washington, D.C.: Corpus Instrumentorum, Inc., 1968.

Manning, Francis V. "The Human Meaning of Sexual Pleasure and the Morality of Premarital Intercourse." <u>American Ecclesiastical Review</u> 165 (September, 1971): 18-28; 166 (January, 1972): 3-21; 166 (May, 1972): 302-319.

May, William E. "Sexuality and Fidelity in Marriage." *Communio* (U.S.) 5 (Fall, 1978): 275-293.

------. "Natural Law." *New Catholic Encyclopedia*. 1967 ed.

McCormick, S.J., Richard. "Ambiguity in Moral Choice." 1973 Pere Marquette Theology Lecture, Marquette University Press.

McGinnis, I. "Sin." *New Catholic Encyclopedia*. 1967 ed.

Milhaven, S.J., John G. "Toward an Epistemology of Ethics." *Theological Studies* 27 (June, 1966): 228-241.

------. "Objective Moral Evaluation of Consequences." *Theological Studies* 32 (September, 1971): 407-430.

O'Shea, C.SS.R., Kevin F. "The Reality of Sin: A Theological and Pastoral Critique." *Theological Studies* 29 (June, 1968): 241-259.

Paul VI. "Address to the Society of Italian Catholic Jurists." In *Love and Sexuality*. Edited by Odile M. Liebard. Wilmington, North Carolina: McGrath Publishing Company, 1978, pp. 389-392.

Pius XII. "Address to the Italian Medical-Biological Union of St. Luke." In *Love and Sexuality*, pp. 84-95. Edited by Odile M. Liebard. Wilmington, North Carolina: McGrath Publishing Company, 1978.

Rahner, S.J., Karl. "Dogmatic Reflections on the Knowledge and Self-Consciousness of Christ." In *Theological Investigations* 5. Translated by Karl H. Kruger. (Baltimore: Helicon Press, 1966), pp. 193-215.

Ryan, Columba. "The Traditional Concept of Natural Law: An Interpretation." In *Light on the Natural Law*, pp. 13-37. Edited by I. Evans. Baltimore: Helicon, 1965.

Schuller, S.J., Bruno. "Direct Killing/Indirect Killing." In *Readings in Moral Theology No. 1: Moral Norms and Catholic Tradition*, pp. 138-157. Edited by Charles E. Curran and Richard McCormick, S.J. New York: Paulist Press, 1979.

Simons, Francis. "The Catholic Church and the New Morality." *Cross Currents* 16 (1966): 429-445.

Smith, William B. "Morality and Sexuality, What the Church Teaches." In *Human Sexuality in Our Times*, pp. 148-171. Edited by Msgr. George A. Kelly. Boston: Daughters of St. Paul, 1979.

Springer, S.J., Robert H. "Conscience, Behavioral Science and Absolutes." In *Absolutes in Moral Theology?*, pp. 19-56. Edited by Charles E. Curran. Washington, D.C." Corpus Instrumentorum, Inc., 1968.

Vatican II. "Decree on Priestly Formation." The Documents of Vatican II, pp. 437-457. Edited By Walter M. Abbott, S.J. Translated by Joseph Gallagher. New York: Corpus Instrumentorium Inc., 1966.

------. "Pastoral Constitution on the Church in the Modern World." The Documents of Vatican II, pp. 199-308. Edited by Walter M. Abbott, S.J. Translated by Joseph Gallagher. New York: Corpus Instrumentorum, Inc., 1966.

von Hildebrand, Dietrich. Morality and Situation Ethics. Chicago: Franciscan Herald Press, 1966.

C. Unpublished Works

Connery, S.J., John R. "The Morality of Incomplete Venereal Pleasure." S.T.D. Dissertation, Gregorian University, 1948.

Friday, Rev. Robert M. "Adults Making Responsible Moral Decisions." National Conference of Diocesan Directors of Religious Education Resource Paper, 1979.

McCormick, S.J., Richard. "De Sexto Mandato." Class notes. West Baden College, 1961.

Name and Subject Index

A

Abbott, S.J., Walter 91
Acquaviva, S.J., Claude 14-15, 18, 25, 34, 37, 82, 83, 84, 86, 97, 101
Aertnys, C.SS.R., J. 37-38, 43, 79, 92
Alexander VII 22, 32, 83, 85, 86
Alszeghy, S.J., Z. 65
Aquinas, St. Thomas 4, 5, 9, 10, 11, 24, 26, 39, 51, 54, 58, 98, 108, 113
Aranjo, P. 3, 17
Augustine, St. 57, 65, 98, 110, 112, 113

B

Belliveau, Fred 112
Benedict XIV 84
Billuart, O.P., Charles-Rene 19-22, 25
Brouillard, R. 28
Brown, S.S., Raymond E. 113

C

Cajetan, Thomas 22, 23, 30
Caramuel (de Lobkowitz) Juan 16-17, 25, 28
Carroll, William 77-80, 110, 113
Clement VIII 18, 36, 42, 82
Commentary on the Second
  Book of the Sentences 9
Connery, S.J., John 3, 4, 7, 82-83, 85, 92, 93
Council of Trent 100
Cunningham, SSCM, Agnes 77-80, 110, 113
Curran, Charles E. 4, 8, 9, 12, 27, 45, 47-49, 50, 51, 60, 62, 63, 66, 75-76, 91

D

Damen, C.SS.R., C.A. 37-38, 43, 79, 92
Davis, S.J., Henry 3, 4, 8, 35-37, 41, 43, 76
de Arriaga, S.J., Roderico 16
de Cardenas, S.J., Juan 17-18, 19, 25
Declaration on Sexual Ethics 4, 76, 82, 84, 90, 107, 112
De Malo 10, 11
Denziger, H. 30, 43, 92
Diana, Antonius 22
Dogmatic Constitution on
  Divine Revelation 80
Doherty, Dennis J. 65, 113
Duhamel, S.J., J. 85
Dulles, S.J., Avery 8

F

Fagan, S.J., Sean   63, 65, 66
Flick, S.J., M.   65
Fransen, S.J., Pierre   64
Friday, Rev. Robert M.   62
Fuchs, S.J., Joseph   49-50, 54, 63, 64, 65, 67, 68, 72-74,
                      80-81, 85, 90, 91, 92
Fumo, B.   3
Fundamental Option   54, 59, 60, 61, 68, 72-74

G

Gallagher, Joseph   91
Gaudium et Spes   1, 95
Gelin, A.   64
Genicot, S.J., Edward   8, 31-32, 41, 68, 90
Glaser, John W.   56, 65

H

Haring, C.SS.R., Bernard   47, 64, 71-72, 90
Hart, T.   64
Hartmann, L.   64
Hirscher, John Baptist   47
Humanae Vitae   1, 85, 95

J

Janssens, Louis   54, 63
John XXIII, Pope   49
Johann, S.J., Robert O.   63
Jone, O.F.M. Cap., Heribert   8

K

Keane, S.S., Philip S.   64, 68-70, 112
Kleber, Karl-Heinz   4, 8, 26
Koch, R.   64
Kosnik, Anthony   77-80, 110, 113

L

Lacroix, S.J., Claudius   18-19, 29
Lauras, Dr. Andre   112
Ledesma   3
Liguori, Alphonsus   22-23, 25, 31
Lonergan, S.J., Bernard   64
Lyonnet, S.   64

M

Magister, Martinus 3, 10-12, 17, 24-25, 27
Maguire, Daniel 8, 74, 91
Manualists 2, 5, 31, 40-41, 42, 47, 51, 53, 54, 60, 68, 70, 74, 75, 76
Manya, Joanne 58, 65
Marchant, J. 3, 17
Martin of Azpilcueta
  (Doctor Navarrus) 12, 13, 22, 23, 27
Mater et Magistra 112
May, William E. 63
McCormick, S.J., Richard 54, 64, 65, 84, 85, 93, 107-108, 113
McDonagh, E. 65
McGinnis, I. 8
Merkelbach, O.P., Benedict H. 38-40, 44, 79, 92
Metz, J. 65
Milhaven, John 53, 63, 72, 91
Modras, Ronald 77-80, 110, 113
Monden, L. 65

N

Noldin, S.J., H. 8, 32-34, 41, 42, 84, 92

O

O'Callaghan, D. 64
O'Connell, Timothy E. 63, 68, 87
O'Shea, C.SS.R., Kevin 59, 64, 66

P

Paul V, Pope 18, 36, 42, 82, 84
Paul VI, Pope 112
Pius XII, Pope 112
Proposition 40 32, 36, 38, 40, 41

R

Rahner, S.J., Karl 64
Regan, C.M., George M. 47-48, 62
Richter, Lin 112

S

Sacra Virginitas   112
Sacred Congregation for the
  Doctrine of the Faith   4, 8, 84, 92, 93, 112
Sailer, John Michael   47
Salamanca Theologians   22, 23
Sanchez, S.J., Thomas   12-14, 17, 22, 23, 24, 82, 92
Schmitt, S.J., A.   8, 32-34, 84, 92
Schoenmetzer, A.   30, 43, 92
Schoonenberg, S.J., Piet   64
Schuller, Bruno   54, 57, 64, 65
Scriptum Super Libros Sententiarum   26
Simons, Francis   63
Sin   2-3
Smith, William B.   80, 92
Springer, S.J., Robert   46-47
Summa Theologia   9, 26, 27

T

Tamburinus, Thomas   22
Tanner, S.J., Adam   16
Tubingen School   47

V

van der Marck, William   63
Vatican II   1, 2, 5, 31, 42, 49, 50, 67, 77, 80, 99, 102, 111